This book is dedicated
to the following past and present Members of

NORTHWESTERN UNIVERSITY

with thanks for the many hours of discussion
whereof these pages are the fruit

RICHARD C. ADAMS  ROBERT BUSCH
PRISCILLA CLARK  ALBERT CRAIG
DOROTHY M. DEWITT  FERDINAND FENDER
CARLTON GAMER  EMERSON R. HARRIS
ROSEMARY HODGINS  GLORIA A. LOVE
STEELE W. MARTIN  ROSE ADAMEK MCGEE
MURIEL PINDER PISCHEL  ROBERT H. PLATMAN
DONALD H. POTTS  WINIFRED STENE
CLARRA MAE SULLIVAN

# THE
# SUPREME IDENTITY

*An Essay*
*on Oriental Metaphysic and*
*the Christian Religion*

by
ALAN WATTS

## VINTAGE BOOKS
### A Division of Random House, New York

VINTAGE BOOKS EDITION   September, 1972
Preface Copyright © 1972 by Alan Watts

Library of Congress Cataloging in Publication Data
Watts, Alan Wilson, 1915–   , The supreme identity.
Reprint of the 1950 ed.      Bibliography: pp. 195-99
    1. Christianity and other religions.
        2. Religion—Philosophy.
    3. Philosophy, Oriental. I. Title.
    [BR127.W3 1972]   201   72–3410
        ISBN 0–394–71835–6 (pbk.)

# CONTENTS

# PREFACE
## TO THE NEW EDITION

It must be remembered that I wrote this book in 1949, just at the time when I was about to cease my official connection as a priest of the Anglican Communion, and had not entirely made up my mind to do so. Thus, in retrospect, its argument seems to me somewhat tortuous, though because there is nevertheless much in it which still seems to me to be valid, we are putting out a new and very slightly revised edition. It was written rather specifically for theologians and students of comparative religion, and is thus—along with *The Way of Zen*—one of the more serious and scholarly books that I have written. However, my present position with respect to the Catholic tradition remains as explained in *Beyond Theology* (1964) and in the Preface to the New Edition of *Behold the Spirit* (1971), and there is no point in repeating it here.

In the original Preface to *The Supreme Identity* I said that, as a philosopher, I was neither trying to lay down the law nor to defend a consistent position, but simply to initiate a friendly and intelligent discussion with other theologians about Christianity *vis à vis* Vedanta and Buddhism. The response was originally terse and disgruntled, but in time it really got going—in particular with such delightful churchmen as Bishop James Pike and Paul Tillich, Bishop John A. T. Robinson, Dom Aelred Graham O.S.B., Father Heinrich Dumoulin S.J., Dean Charles U. Harris, Brother David O.S.B., and many others who seem to me to represent a new and vigorous Christianity which feels no need to minimize the insights of other spiritual traditions, but rather to see them as incorporate in the Body of Christ.

I have been trying almost all my life to work for a true catholicity, a fellowship wherein Christians, Hindus, Buddhists, Muslims, Taoists, Jews, and the rest could recognize their common Ground, and worship or meditate together without quarrelling, and yet without abandoning their interesting and colorful differences of method and style. I would not really want to see a Buddha-image on the high altar of St. Peter's or a crucifix in the Kaaba, but it is being increas-

7

ingly recognized that at the level of contemplative mysticism (or what in this book is called 'metaphysic') there is no essential difference between Zen Buddhists, Sufis, Vedantists, and blessedly silent Trappists. For when one gets into the domain of pure contemplation of the Ground of Being, there is no more talk going on inside the head, and therefore no occasion for disputation. There is simply a consciousness clear as crystal and open to truth, reality, or what is—which, as St. Thomas Aquinas would have said, is what all men call God.

Historically, the Jews, Christians, and Muslims have been the most disputatious religionists of all, largely because of their excessive dependence on the authority of holy scriptures and their relative neglect of non-verbal forms of worship. But among Christians, excepting perhaps the lunatic fringe of Protestant fundamentalists, it is being increasingly recognized that the Word or Logos of God is not to be confused with the specifically spelled-out directions of written or spoken language. The Word of God is obviously non-linear, for it would be impossible to govern all the simultaneous and multitudinous operations of this universe by commandments giving out one 'bit' of information at a time. This was why St. Paul explained that whereas the spirit gives life the letter kills, and Jesus reproached the Pharisees saying, 'You search the scriptures daily, for in them you *think* you have life.'

It is thus that the revelation given to Israel is not the only revelation that has ever been given. Supposing that there are human beings on other planets in this or other galaxies: must they wait for missionaries from Earth to have redemption through Moses, or Christ, or Mohammed? Similarly, what opportunity for salvation was there for Chinese, Incas, and Australians while Jesus was living in Palestine, in a world absolutely out of communication with theirs? Surely, if it is true that God so loves the world, and means it, he will give his only-begotten Son in as many forms as there are worlds. Furthermore, when it is said that there is no other Name under heaven whereby men may be saved than the Name of Jesus, it should always have been understood that the Name of Jesus is not the proper name JESUS (or Joshua, or Aissa, or Iesous) but the *spirit* of Jesus—which is to say the Second Person of the Trinity, the Logos, the Only-Begotten Son, and (in feminine aspect) the Sophia or Wisdom of God. There is

8

*the Sophia*

absolutely nothing in Catholic dogmatics, or even in the Bible, to compel anyone to believe that Jesus of Nazareth was the one and only incarnation of the Only-Begotten Son in all time and space.

To many people—even devout Catholics—these problems of biblical and ecclesiastical authority are ceasing to have much meaning. But what has been happening in the last twenty years, and what this book was intended to encourage, is that—without all the rigmarole of official councils and concordats—very learned and holy Christians have entered into spiritual fellowship with comparable representatives of other traditions without trying to convert them. Jesuit and Benedictine priests have been practicing Zen and Yoga, and the Trappist, Thomas Merton, had the finest understanding of Zen of almost any Western interpreter.[1]

My many friends, old and new, among the clergy have become less frantic and strident in their doctrine, not because of a merely sentimental desire for œcumenicity, but because of a remarkable deepening of their own interior lives which must have come about, at least in some measure, from this spiritual meeting of the East and the West. Things have come to such a point that I could almost function again as a Christian priest, except that I think I can communicate with more people as a loner and outsider who—very obviously—does not represent the vested interests of any religious organization.

It has, furthermore, become my conviction that partisanship in religion is no longer intellectually respectable, and that the various religions should be regarded as differing styles of doing the same thing.

Since writing *The Supreme Identity* I have travelled over much of the world and have witnessed the religious observances of many traditions. It has struck me that if one pays no attention to the meanings of the word, most forms of temple-doings are essentially the same: chanting, bowing, candles, incense, gongs, and bells—from the peyote ritual of the Ogalala Sioux to the Russian Orthodox Cathedral of Paris, and from the Abbey of San Anselmo in Rome to the Daitoku Temple in Kyoto. If you understand the point of the Zen story about Ping-ting on page 192, it will be obvious why

---

[1] See especially his essay *The Zen Revival.*

# PREFACE TO THE NEW EDITION

there are instances in which getting the word (or sound) is more important than getting the meaning. Remember that as a little child, when you hardly understood what adults were saying, you saw with incredible clarity what they were doing —not in terms of moral evaluation but in terms of 'the particular go of it'. This is why one must become again as a child to enter the kingdom of heaven, and also why a Buddha is called a *tathagata*, that is, one who comes or goes 'thus'. In silence of the mind, in which one is simply aware of 'what is' without comment, all believers can suspend their opinions and together contemplate reality. If I resolve that final phrase into its original form, it means 'to gather within the temple [to observe] the thing itself'.

ALAN WATTS

*Sausalito, California*
*March 1972*

# PREFACE
## TO THE FIRST EDITION

We must face certain facts about the spiritual state of our civilization. One, too obvious to need much stress, is that in practice our religious and educational institutions are providing neither the wisdom nor the power to cope with the political, economic and psychological predicament in which we find ourselves. There can now be little doubt that, if it follows its present course, the final result of Western man's 'conquest of nature', scientific progress, and cultural imperialism will be a 'last state worse than the first', worse than the supposed barbarism in which the history of Europe began. The present condition of Western civilization threatens the world with dangers that far outweigh its many achievements and blessings.

Another fact, far less obvious, is that our cultural expansion has brought us, quite unintentionally, a great spiritual opportunity. While we have been trying to secure our political, economic and cultural rule over the peoples of Asia, we have been quietly but powerfully invaded by the Orient in the realm of the mind. Western thought is beginning to feel the influence of what we call oriental 'philosophy and religion', though so long as we can believe that this influence is confined to a few scholars or to cultists and faddists, we are not going to be seriously concerned. Every day, however, we are hearing more and more about 'the contribution of the ancient East to modern culture'. Yet while thoughtful Westerners are agreed that we do have something to learn from the wisdom of the East, they are mostly of the opinion that it is little more than a refining enrichment of our already far superior way of life.

In view of the disastrous state into which our way of life seems to be leading, Western man's cocksureness of his spiritual and cultural superiority is amazing. While this might be expected of those of us who do not believe in spirituality, of our humanists and rationalists who deem the secularism of the modern world a good, it is tragic indeed to find the same attitude among most leaders of the Christian religion. Indeed, the fear and incomprehension which so many of them show towards oriental wisdom

II

is one of the most important signs of our spiritual weakness and blindness.

The time has come for Christians to take the spiritual traditions of Asia seriously, to recognize that their presence among us is nothing less than providential, to understand and come to terms with them. This does not call for any doctrinal alteration of Christianity or for any 'merging of religions in a common faith', because, as will be shown in the following chapters, spiritual traditions such as the Vedanta, Buddhism and Taoism are not religions in the strict sense, and cannot be regarded as competing with Christianity.

The wisdom which Asia has to offer embodies not only the human mind's most profound understanding of life, but also a knowledge essential to human order and sanity. In some of my former works, notably *Behold the Spirit*, I have tried to show how this wisdom might, as it were, be woven into the fabric of Christianity. I have come to see, however, that such interweaving is unsatisfactory, for 'no man putteth new cloth into old garments'. Christianity needs no additions or amplifications from outside, and the attempt to incorporate any oriental doctrine within it, as if the two kinds of doctrine were of the same order, is merely confusing. It is like trying to interpolate fragments of a symphony into the midst of a dance. Properly, the two should be set side by side, and related by analogy instead of mixture.

Despite the fact that in *Behold the Spirit* I tried to avoid mixture by distinguishing between the form and the meaning of dogma, the device was not wholly successful. For it is so generally assumed that the meaning of dogma is already the concern of theology, that it looked as if I were trying to introduce a strange theology, if not a strange dogma. Many people felt, therefore, that the introduction of a certain type of mysticism into the structure of Christian theology threatened to break that structure, to annihilate its essential historical and sacramental emphasis. I believe that this criticism was to some extent justified.

But this kind of confusion has a long history. It is not only that in recent years we have tried to understand oriental traditions as religions and theologies comparable to our own—to our immense befuddlement. It is also that certain remnants of these traditions have, through Greek sources, penetrated Christian theology from the earliest times, and have never been properly assimilated and understood. For example, the strict concept of eternity as timelessness rather than everlastingness is such a remnant. We have tried to incorporate this and similar concepts in our theology, in a single framework of doctrine, without understanding that this is trying to speak two utterly different languages at once. A theology dealing with dogmatic, historical and sacramental ideas is an approach to Reality utterly distinct from a 'metaphysical mysticism'. The two kinds of language cannot be mixed without hopeless confusion—a confusion which lies at the root of the major difficulties of theological thought. Furthermore, the fact that Western man has not perceived this difference is the result of a certain 'metaphysical blindness', which, as I shall try to show, is the most serious weakness of our civilization.

For there is a realm of spiritual wisdom which religion as we know it can express by analogy only. When we try to speak of it more directly, we must go beyond religious language, beyond the forms of thought which dogma, sacrament and theology can legitimately employ. It is a wisdom which neither conflicts with nor supersedes religion, because it is in some sense outside the religious sphere. Its province is a mystery with which religion, as such, is not *directly* concerned, and about which it has no official teaching, since it cannot be expressed directly in the religious type of language. But though it lies beyond the religious sphere, religion interprets it as a dancer interprets music. This is, however, a music to which we are very largely deaf, for which reason most of us must rely on religion for the only connection with it which, in this life, we can have. Yet if the dance of religion is to proceed with spirit and strength, at least the leaders of the dance must hear the tune.

In itself this wisdom has a glory which absolutely defies description. But the only human language which can discuss it at all intelligently and directly is, by comparison with religious language, arid and cold. It is a negative language which employs such almost unthinkable concepts as strict infinity and eternity. It tries to express that inner depth of consciousness which is not accessible to thought and feeling because it lies behind them. This is the language used in that most fundamental text of Catholic mysticism, the *Theologia Mystica* of St. Dionysius, the language of that 'cloud of unknowing', where, beyond the warmth, the passion and the consolations of religious imagery, the utmost peak of man's being touches the infinite.

# PREFACE TO THE FIRST EDITION

In this realm religious and theological distinctions are transcended, though not annihilated. Here Christian and Hindu speak one strange tongue, which we must be most careful not to confuse with the terminology of official theology and scripture.

Difficult and dark from excess of light as this realm may be, it is no exotic bypath of the spirit of little importance for mankind as a whole. On the contrary, it is here that man actually realizes his ultimate meaning and destiny. If only relatively few ever reach this point at any one time, they anchor the rest of us to eternal sanity. A society or a church which has no central place for them, which fears their doctrine and hides their light, is spiritually dead.

Though this wisdom is much less prevalent in Asia than many suppose, it is (or was) at least respected. But in our own ecclesiastical circles those who show any interest in it are usually regarded as eccentric and a little mad, and sometimes as dangerous heretics. But when religion ignores this vital centre of man's spiritual life and treats it as *eccentric*, the Church necessarily falls into impotence and disunity. It loses its own true centre. Thus Christians are now trying to effect reunion and to restore the spiritual power of the Church by a whirl of activity on the mere circumference of things. This activity may be important and necessary, but when unrelated to the vital centre it is almost completely useless. There is not that metaphysical certainty and that profound sense of proportion and meaning, without which the problems of theology and morals dividing Christians from themselves and from the world cannot be seen in their true light.

It is exceedingly difficult to explain this wisdom in words that do not confuse it with theological and philosophical '-isms' to which it bears no resemblance. Indeed, it is so hard to express it in writing at all, that one who tries can only feel acutely conscious of the defects of his effort. But the tragedy of a confused, weakened and sincerely alarmed Christian people ignoring the most essential source of spiritual power, makes it necessary to try. I do not pretend to have expressed such an ultimate mystery at all adequately, nor to have solved all the many hard problems of its relation to Church and society. One man in one lifetime could never cope with such a task, and I offer my work that others may improve upon it. No one should try to make any understanding of these matters his own property and achievement.

I am not one who believes that it is any necessary virtue in the philosopher to spend his life defending a consistent position. It is surely a kind of spiritual pride to refrain from 'thinking out loud', and to be unwilling to let a thesis appear in print until you are prepared to champion it to the death. Philosophy, like science, is a social function, for a man cannot think rightly alone, and the philosopher must publish his thought as much to learn from criticism as to contribute to the sum of wisdom. If, then, I sometimes make statements in an authoritative and dogmatic manner, it is for the sake of clarity rather than from the desire to pose as an oracle.

Since writing *Behold the Spirit* I have been greatly helped by the work of two writers who have, in certain respects, profoundly changed my understanding of the scope and nature of the oriental doctrines and their relation to Christianity—Réné Guénon and the late Ananda Coomaraswamy. I want to take this opportunity of expressing my indebtedness to these two men. At the same time, it is only fair to them to say that while the present work shows their influence, it does not claim in any way to be a faithful representation of their views upon all the subjects discussed.

I want also to insert a note of thanks for the great stimulation which this work has received from Dr. F. S. C. Northrop's *Meeting of East and West*, and from his thoughtful criticism, in correspondence, of the position of *Behold the Spirit*. While there are major points in which I find myself unable to agree with him, his work has helped me to see some of the problems involved much more clearly.

It is a pleasure, too, to acknowledge the help and criticism which this work has received from my wife, and from some of my students who have read the manuscript, notably Mr. Carlton Gamer, Miss Dorothy DeWitt, and Mrs. Carl Pischel, as well as from several others who have discussed the material with me at considerable length, and by their questions helped me to clarify so many points of the argument.

My thanks are also due to Messrs. Charles Scribner's Sons, of New York, and to Geoffrey Bles, of London, for their kind permission to make certain quotations from the works of Nicholas Berdyaev.

ALAN WATTS

*Evanston, Illinois*
*Autumn 1949*

# INTRODUCTION

## OUTLINE

1. Modern civilization is disintegrating because it has no principle of unity, no certain or even workable knowledge of the meaning and true end of human life.

Philosophy and science do not offer such a principle, nor even the hope of finding one, since this is not their proper sphere.

Religion contains our nearest approach to a principle of unity, but does not convince or convert the modern world because its doctrines, as stated, seem incredible.

Societies with a principle of unity have existed, and are more stable and significant than our own, because related consciously to an eternal Reality.

2. (a) The spiritual leadership of a stable and unified society of this kind must have access to *metaphysical* knowledge, i.e., to an effective realization and immediate experience of the ultimate Reality.

Religion offers an analogy of this knowledge, but of this modern Christianity is not aware. Analogy alone collapses when pressed too far, and Christianity is now ineffective and uncertain because it is a hard-pressed analogy trying to stand on its own merits. It lacks the support of the metaphysical knowledge which it represents.

   (b) A discussion of characteristic objections to this thesis:

     i. That knowledge of the infinite is not real knowledge, having no positive content.

    ii. That such knowledge is socially ineffective.

   iii. That such knowledge does not really exist.

# INTRODUCTION

Modern philosophy, science, and even religion seem to have lost hope and, all too often, interest itself in the possibility of metaphysical knowledge. By knowledge of this kind we mean neither religious belief, philosophical speculation, nor scientific theory. We mean actual experience or immediate realization of that ultimate Reality which is the ground and cause of the universe, and thus the principle and meaning of human life.

There are many who think it proper humility for man to disclaim the possibility of this knowledge. Yet we shall try to show not only that such knowledge has existed among men, but also that the modern world's loss of contact with its sources is the chief reason for our culture's peculiar and dangerous disintegration. More important still, we shall try to describe the nature of this knowledge in as far as language will permit, and also the teaching of its principal exponents about the way in which it is realized. However preposterous this may sound to modern ears, we should remember that for other great cultures and times than our own, a venture into this realm would have seemed both necessary and normal.

The reader is warned, therefore, that this subject is more easily misunderstood than any other, not because of technical complexity, but because of unfamiliarity. For this kind of knowledge, and its consequent ways of life and thought, are so strange to the present civilization of the West, that they are far removed from the usual patterns of our thinking and the assumptions on which these are based. We shall have to use many terms which, though familiar enough in themselves, have in the course of time become changed and confused in meaning. The best will be done to define these terms carefully in their present context, but, even so, the reader is asked to guard against associating them with many of the ideas which they usually denote. When the reader finds any statement difficult to understand, the difficulty will usually be cleared up by reading on. Owing to a certain peculiarity of the subject, it is generally necessary to state principles before explaining them.

# INTRODUCTION

## [i]

Our present civilization quite obviously lacks any unifying principle. The degree of unity which the vague term 'modern civilization' implies is in many ways a 'unity of disunity', the peoples involved being given a superficial coherence by the spread of technology and by common acceptance of certain ways of thought whose very nature is to create further disintegration. Try as one may to prevent that dangerous confusion of the world by some unified political and economic system, the truth is that cultural and social unity are expressions of what may for the moment be called spiritual unity, and cannot exist apart from it. There cannot be order and agreement in the particular spheres of human life unless there is common agreement as to the nature and meaning of life itself.

It is clear that differing political systems have their origin in differing philosophies of life, differing ideas as to man's nature and destiny. The dogmatic relativism and individualism of modern philosophy preclude any agreement whatsoever on universal principles of this order. The prevailing schools of philosophy and scientism are practically unanimous in their agreement that man can have no certain knowledge of ultimate reality, of the cause and meaning of the universe, and that it is in all probability quite idle to pursue such knowledge. Social unity must therefore be sought on the ground of man's common physical nature. All must eat; all must be clothed; all must be harmlessly amused.

In practice, however, common physical needs are inadequate as a basis for unity—to put it mildly. If man is nothing more than a physical being, something like a cow or sheep, it is clearly justifiable to treat him as such. The highest good of the race, or herd, will be the greatest biological happiness of the greatest number, and from this point of view there will be nothing, short of pure sentimentality, to prevent the hygienic elimination of all disturbing minorities and misfits, of all who do not conform to the common (though none the less arbitrary) view of the greatest good. If there are, for the common economic good, wonderfully efficient and sanitary slaughter-houses for ordinary cattle, there will be nothing to prevent the construction of still more technologically effective ones for human cattle. Indeed, this is already the established practice in countries where the

19

strictly physical concept of man's nature is the official state dogma.

Our common biological needs would perhaps unify us if we were merely biological beings. But the notion that we are such is already a *philosophy*, or, more exactly, merely one of many uncertain and inconclusive philosophical opinions concerning which the philosophers are already agreed that there can be no agreement. To conceive that his needs are merely biological man has to philosophize. The moment one theory of human life is proposed, there are equally rational grounds for proposing another. As soon as we philosophize we are asking what man is for, what end or ends his physical existence serves. Whether we decide that it merely serves itself, or the abstract glory of the state, or art, or literature, or God, we are at once transferring the entire problem into the realm of ends. Immediately, then, the important thing about human life, the thing upon which human unity will have to be based, is the *end* for which man eats, drinks, amuses himself, and exists. If we cannot agree about this, we cannot be socially united. Common physical needs provide no more basis for unity than the mere power and desire to walk determine where one will go. To say that there is nowhere special to go, or that existing is just for the sake of existing, securely and comfortably, is merely to set oneself at variance with those who, with good reason, may hold other views. In this event the fact that you both need to eat will in no way settle an extremely crucial difference, as to the goal of life.

Man's biological unity is merely an instrumental unity. All have the same instruments, but their life consists in what they do with them. Thus to be united in action we must agree about ends, which means that we must agree philosophically. To agree to differ, to let everyone follow quite independent or contradictory views of man's end, is merely to agree *not* to have any true social union, and to let our society disintegrate spiritually as it is in fact now doing. To agree that we must all eat, drink, and live at peace is still not to agree about ends, about any significant principle of unity. To agree not to philosophize at all, which is the only way to have unity on the purely animal level, is quite impossible since such a decision is already the philosophical opinion of agnosticism. Man is by nature a philosopher, and cannot be otherwise.

It should thus be obvious that modern man's urgent desire

and need for social unity, coupled with despair of or actual antagonism to philosophical agreement, presents a gigantic contradiction. To work for peace and order on the purely political or economic level may be effective in certain subordinate instances, but to work exclusively or even primarily at this level is about as unrealistic a procedure as may be imagined. A society which cannot agree what man is for, which cannot be unanimous in some philosophy of man's true destiny, cannot be a united society.

To modern liberalism the idea of a spiritually unanimous society seems both impossible and undesirable. It suggests the ecclesiastical totalitarianism of the Middle Ages and the restriction of man's liberty of thought. But liberty of thought is not an end in itself, and if pursued for its own sake results in utter confusion. Thought is free to discover reality, to find out what man is for. Liberalism must face the plain fact that if we do not know what man is for, we can neither educate him nor heal his infirmities. If you do not know what an automobile is for, it is absurd to think that you can run or repair it intelligently.

To educate man merely to earn his living in harmony with others is simply giving him the power to live without a goal, and even without any principle of harmony. It is to set him going just for the sake of going, with the request that he help others to go also, and not get in their way. But when no one knows *where* he is going—except to some place where he can just keep on going—the result is a confusion and futility which no amount of well-meaning liberalism can control. Man needs somewhere to go. We must ask, then, whether there is any hope that modern philosophy, science and religion may provide an answer.

Thus far we have used the word 'philosophy' in an extremely loose sense, a sense which might include religion, mysticism, patriotism, or any other mode of expressing the meaning of life, as well as philosophy properly so called. Modern academic philosophy, the discipline of logic, epistemology, ontology, and the like, is about as far as it could be from providing modern society with any principle of unity. Sincere and brilliant as its disciples may be, it would be difficult to find a group more uncertain and confused in its collective mind.

It goes without saying that such uncertainty reflects open and honest minds which shun hasty and prejudiced conclusions. But we shall see that in confining itself to logic, and to the realms of aesthetic and sensory experience, philosophy is restricted to a wholly contingent sphere which can never produce a universal, as distinct from a merely general, principle of the kind required. Absorbed in contingencies, modern philosophy has the disunity of mere contingencies. So far from looking to it for a principle of unity, society tucks philosophy away in obscure corners of its universities, retaining it only as an academic hobby. Modern philosophy is a corpus of ingenious but wholly inconclusive speculation, uncertain of the very methods of logic and cognition which it employs. We shall see, however, that for all its academic seclusion, it exercises a powerful but largely confusing influence upon the world.

Although the phrase 'scientific truth' has for our age almost the same ring of ultimate authority as the phrase 'Catholic truth' had for the past, the honest and strict scientist is the last person to claim such authority. As a human being, every scientist is a philosopher; but he is not a philosopher as a scientist. As a scientist he is vividly aware of the limitations of his branch of knowledge. He knows that science is the measurement, description and classification of natural processes; it is the study of *how* things behave. It cannot tell *what* things are, nor *why* they behave. It describes life in operation, but does not presume to say what life is for. The scientist has somewhat the same relation to the philosopher as the grammarian to the poet. The grammarian classifies the various words in a poem, identifies them as nouns, verbs or adjectives, and describes their syntactical relation to one another. He judges the poem grammatical or ungrammatical, but he does not presume to say whether it is good or bad poetry either in respect to the beauty of the words employed or in respect to the sense conveyed. It is therefore a most serious abuse of science to attempt to make it produce a philosophy of life. This it can no more provide than the study of grammar can supply meanings to be expressed in words.

'In our endeavour to understand reality we are somewhat like a man trying to understand the mechanism of a closed watch. He sees the face and the moving hands, even hears its ticking, but he has no way of opening the case. If he is ingenious he may form some picture of a mechanism which could be responsible for all the things he observes, but he may never be quite sure his picture is the only one which could explain his observations. He will never be able to compare his picture with the real mechanism and he cannot even imagine the possibility or the meaning of such a comparison.'[1]

Or, as a confession of the limitations of science, we may cite the more succinct comment of Sir Arthur Eddington on the mystery of the electron, 'Something unknown is doing we don't know what'.

The quasi-religious authority popularly given to science will be as little welcomed by scientists themselves as the exaggerated hopes for social peace and order which are likewise entrusted to such applications of science as psychology and technology. The actual danger of purely technological progress is sufficiently clear in the shape of the atomic bomb to need no further stress. And in so far as psychology is a physiology of the soul, it has no more to say on the destiny of the soul than a doctor has to say about the destination of the body on a given walk. Psychologists may heal sick souls and doctors sick bodies, but, *in so far as they are pure scientists*, they will have no idea as to what healthy souls and bodies are for.[2] The sole function of science in relation to the realm of ends is to determine, as far as may be possible, what uses of soul and body are actually harmful to them, though even here there are occasions when the end will be sufficient to justify damage, perhaps death, to the body for reasons quite outside the scientific sphere. A physician, acting solely as such, would hardly have advised Christ to be crucified.

Whereas, academic philosophy simply fails to provide human society with any principle of unity, science is not even intended or equipped to do so. Its function is as strictly instrumental as man's physical nature. So far as science is concerned, scientists themselves have in recent years made so many pronouncements upon the strict limitations of their field of knowledge that the point needs no further emphasis.

For purposes of this brief and preliminary survey of the possible sources of a principle of unity, it remains to consider religion. A religion with universal claims, such as Christianity,

[1] Einstein and Infeld, *The Evolution of Physics* (Cambridge, 1938), p. 33.
[2] Thus it is doubtful whether a successful psychotherapist can ever remain a pure scientist. To the extent that the health of the soul depends upon its being diverted to some end, the psychologist must be a philosopher.

regards the unification of the human race in its true end, God, as its supreme function, and for several centuries the Catholic Faith did actually provide Western society with a principle of unity. Christendom was indeed, with quite minor exceptions, a philosophically unanimous culture which, despite the family feuds of princes, gave Europe such coherence as remains to it even in its present disintegration.

With certain important reservations, it would seem to be true that Catholicism in some form is the only likely vehicle of a unifying principle that remains in the Western world. For, popularly speaking, modern Protestantism has become so vague, uncertain and confused in matters of doctrine that its only bond, as well as its only teaching, is a morality based on external imitation of the personal conduct of Jesus. It should be easy to see that a common morality is far from a true principle of unity. To be sure, it is a somewhat more adequate bond than the mere commonalty of means and instruments rather than ends.

If morality consists in doing good to one's fellow-man, it is clear that morality exists for man rather than man for morality, and the problem of what man himself is for is still undecided. If I live simply in order to serve my brother, what is my brother going to do with the service I give him? Serve me? Does the race exist just to serve itself, and if so to *what* shall it serve itself? To food and clothes for all, to information, medication and harmless amusements? Mere morality as the unifying principle brings us back dangerously close to the biological ideal of the greatest good of the greatest number. Of itself, it offers no real reason for the respect of minorities because it rests on no doctrine as to the true nature of the human person. Its motives for mutual goodwill are purely sentimental, having no deeper origin than fellow-feeling and pity on the positive side, and, on the negative side, that ingrained sense of guilt sometimes called the 'New England' or 'Nonconformist' conscience.

On the other hand, Catholicism and some of the more old-fashioned though less influential types of Protestantism have a real doctrine of the meaning of human life, namely that man's true end is union with God in the contemplation of the Beatific Vision. Of all ideas as to the ultimate destiny of man this alone, quite apart from any question of its truth, gives us a real end, a point beyond which the question of further purpose cannot be asked, because the enjoyment of God is an *infinite* good.

# INTRODUCTION

'All other human operations seem to be ordered to this as to their end. For perfect contemplation requires that the body should be disencumbered, and to this effect are directed all the products of art that are necessary for life. Moreover, it requires freedom from the disturbance caused by passions, which is achieved by means of the moral virtues and of prudence; and freedom from external disturbance, to which the whole governance of civil life is directed. So that, if we consider the matter rightly, we shall see that all human occupations appear to serve those who contemplate the truth. . . . Man's ultimate happiness consists solely in the contemplation of God.'[1]

Yet such a statement of the final cause of human life and society is wholly foreign to the modern mind, which regards the contemplation of God as a selfish and anti-social ideal beloved of escapists who cannot face the challenge of reality—a challenge which presumably consists in becoming so involved in the moral and physical 'improvement' of mankind that one has neither time nor energy to wonder where such improvement is supposed to lead, and is thus unable to judge whether it is actually improvement.

But it should be obvious by now that the real escapist, the real obscurantist who balks the realization of social unity, is precisely the person who will not face the question of man's true end. Of course, the kind of person we have in mind dare not face it. His philosophy of life is so narrow and impoverished that he can see no end beyond the extinction of our sparks of consciousness in oblivion, and he flees the contemplation of this dismal 'reality' by throwing himself into a whirl of superficial agitation and business. He is like the sort of automobile enthusiast who spends so much time dismantling and rebuilding his car that he never drives anywhere.

Unhappily, any general acceptance of the Catholic ideal as the principle of unity has serious obstacles in its way. The more obvious are the corrupt politics and the secularism of the existing Church, and the fact that so large a portion of mankind finds itself unable to believe the doctrines of the Church as they are generally stated. As will be seen in due course, these obstacles are only the surface manifestations of much deeper matters. Indeed, the chances that the modern world as we now

[1] St. Thomas, *Summa Contra Gentiles*, III, xxxvii.

know it will ever find a principle of unity are extremely small. Western culture seems at the moment spiritually disintegrated beyond hope of reconstruction, and perhaps the best that may be expected is that in its final collapse it may give birth to a new culture, much as it had its own origin in the waning Classical culture of the Roman Empire.

Nevertheless, the question of man's true end and of the principle of human unity remains of supreme importance, if not for this present society, for another, and if not for another, for such individuals as feel the urgent need to make sense out of existence. But because, as Toynbee and others have pointed out, new cultures have a way of beginning in the very midst of the old, and since the present age may thus be a time of both death and gestation, the birth of any new culture from the ruins of the old will depend on the discovery of some principle of unity. Although considerations of the future are the by-product and not at all the chief concern of the kind of principle we have in mind, it would be fortunate if there could exist at the present time some nuclear group having a principle of unity around which the new society could form, even though it possessed no externally organized character.[1]

A human society with a true principle of unity is no utopian dream, nor yet a panacea for all the ills and problems of man's life. Societies of this kind have already existed, and though their members suffer war, pestilence, famine and violence in common with the whole race of man, there are the best reasons for saying that such societies are far more stable and significant than our own. By 'significant' we mean that they are related to universals. A part is significant when joined to an organic whole greater than itself, and greater than the sum of its parts. In the highest sense, that is significant which is related to the universal and eternal, which finds its true end in the fullness of Infinite Being. It is significant, in a negative sense, that the prevailing philosophy of our most unstable and unrelated age denies or ignores the existence of anything outside the realm of contingency and relativity. Despite the contradiction involved, nothing is per-

---

[1] Such absence of external organization would, indeed, be a positive advantage, for it would make the nucleus impossible to identify by any hostile elements in the old culture. At the same time, we shall see that lack of organization would hardly offer any serious handicap to a nucleus of the right nature.

mitted to be absolute, infinite or eternal save absolute relativism. If the philosophers would apply their own favourite pragmatic test to such theories, their connection with the disintegration of society might cause them to think again.

In speaking of societies with a principle of unity we have in mind such cultures as the Indian, the Chinese, the Egyptian, and, in a lesser sense, Christendom itself. The latter is instructive because so close to us in time and space, though it contained certain peculiar elements which denied it the stability of the others. Of the Egyptian we have so little intimate knowledge that it may only be mentioned in passing. Of the Indian and Chinese we know, or are able to know, a great deal, not least because they are to some extent still present with us.

For the moment, two characteristics of these societies may be noted. The first is that they are what we must call cosmological. That is to say, there is a conscious and deliberate harmony between their arts and institutions and certain universal principles. This harmony is one of analogy, whereby the social order, the conduct of individual life, the arts and the sciences are so many adaptations in various domains of what is known to be the ultimate meaning of life and the true end of man. For example, the Chinese classic known as the *Tao Te Ching* may be read equivalently as a manual of metaphysic, of natural philosophy, of statecraft, or of the conduct of personal life. It is not just that scattered references to all these domains may be found within its covers, but that almost the entire treatise may be read in, say, either a metaphysical or a political sense. To cite another example, the much misunderstood and now degraded caste system of India was based on the perception that society has a threefold order corresponding by analogy to the inner constitution of man (approximating to what Christians term body, soul, and spirit) and to the three cosmological principles of inertia (*tamas*), activity (*rajas*), and balance or equilibrium (*sattva*).[1]

[1] It would involve an extremely long digression to give anything like an adequate account of these cosmological correspondences in oriental society. The reader is therefore referred to A. K. Coomaraswamy's *Religious Basis of the Forms of Indian Society* (New York, 1946), and to his *Spiritual Authority and Temporal Power in the Indian Theory of Government* (New Haven, 1942), and also to E. J. Urwick's *Message of Plato* (London, 1920), wherein the author explores the connection between the *Republic* and the *Laws of Manu*. 'It must be noted', he

# INTRODUCTION

Quite apart from the question of whether these analogical relationships have the least objective reality, or whether they are purely fanciful and arbitrary constructions, we merely cite them as examples of the fact that in some of our more ancient and stable societies every department of life is designedly related to the ultimate meaning and nature of the universe. Man, his institutions, his arts, his labour, is seen as a microcosm inseparably bound up with the macrocosm, an integral part of the universe in which he lives. But the constant and almost unconscious assumption of modern thought in the West, largely produced by the artificial circumstances of urban life, is that man is in some way isolated from his universe, and is able to analyse and criticize it as if the resulting judgments bore no reflection on his own nature. A philosopher can assert that the universe is without any objective meaning, seemingly unaware of the fact that his very idea, as part of that universe, must also be without meaning.

The second characteristic of these societies is that they are traditional. The development (if that word may be used) of their philosophies, arts and sciences cannot satisfactorily be explained by any historical method, as if it involved some kind of progression. In the first place, we have no real information at all as to the origin of their principal sacred writings. We have excellent reasons for believing that they were transmitted orally for an indeterminably long period before they were committed to writing, as well as for supposing that the names of their authors—Manu, Yajnavalkya, Fu-hsi—do not refer to historic persons. In fact their authorship is as anonymous as that of the world's great myths. For it is characteristic of the traditional approach that no doctrine has respect when claimed as the original work of a human individual; such a claim would throw doubt upon its truth. The essence of the type of doctrine concerned is its universality, and an individual would no more

writes,'—and this is characteristic of the extraordinary consistency of the Vedanta doctrine—that every important conception in psychology or ethics or anything else has its counterpart in, or is a form of, a wider conception involved in the explanation of the whole universe and every part of it' (p. 21). For the equivalent in Chinese society, see Alfred Forke's *World-Conception of the Chinese* (London, 1925), and Legge's translation of the *Li Chi* ('Book of Rites'), *SBE* vols. 27 and 28 (Oxford, 1885). Selections from the latter appear in Lin Yutang's *Wisdom of Confucius* (New York, 1943).

dream of laying a claim to it than to the sun or the law of gravity. Thus the authorship is attributed to divine or semi-divine beings.[1]

The same practice is largely true of the arts and sciences, for because they are based on universal principles they are regarded as works of nature rather than man, as bodies of knowledge belonging to no one in particular. The whole idea of innovation is repugnant to the traditional spirit, and whatever may appear to be an innovation is understood as no more than the realization of what had existed from the beginning. Things which appear to be developments are not thought of as improvements so much as variations on a theme, different and equally valid ways of manifesting a traditional principle. The essential mark of traditional societies is therefore that individuals lay no claim to anything of universal truth or application. They look upon them as eternal, and thus as things which anyone might discover at any time. They save themselves the embarrassment of moderns who announce the invention of some great new idea, only to find out later that it was discussed thousands of years ago.

It follows that traditional societies attach a rather small importance to the study of history. For they understand tradition not so much, as in the West, as something handed down from the past, as the handing down of principles from the eternal realm to the temporal. A tradition reaching into the past is simply an analogy of this, and as such its actual history is of little moment. Furthermore, their relatively constant and stable character, coupled with a merciful absence of newspapers and rapid transportation, means that there is not much 'significant' history to record. Apart from a few isolated wonders and disturbances of a sufficiently sensational nature to be distinguished from others, one year, one century, is much like the next.

While we shall have much more to say later of this attitude to history, it is of interest that the Western mind is rather appalled

---

[1] A similar practice has been followed in the Judaeo-Christian tradition. The *Pentateuch* is not the work of Moses, nor the *Proverbs* of Solomon, nor the *Book of Enoch* the work of Enoch, nor the *Theologia Mystica* of Dionysius the Areopagite. No deceit or deliberate forgery is involved in these attributions of authorship, but rather an honest disclaimer of originality in the belief that the subject-matter has been received through tradition or revealed by inspiration.

by the stability and seeming monotony of this non-historical mode of existence. The occidental considers a culture of this type static, in contrast to his own dynamic culture. The sense of monotony is the result of an improper use of memory, and of a constant comparison of the present with the past—a comparison to which Western man is moved by his egotism, by his irresistible itch to be an improvement on all the former generations of mankind. Even a slight appreciation of eternal realities causes men to live chiefly in the present, and thus to increase their power to observe and understand life as it actually lives before them. To say that such a life is not dynamic is to say that the sun, moon, and stars, the oceans and rivers, the whole realm of nature is not dynamic, just because it follows the same patterns of movement (though with countless subtle variations) for untold aeons. There is all the difference in the world between the truly dynamic and the merely agitated—agitation being unprincipled movement for the sake of pure novelty, resulting largely from over-excited nerves.

In the same line of thought, it is becoming more and more obvious that the supposed superiority of 'progressive' Western society over the 'unprogressive' societies of the East, is rather dubious. Our progress has been almost exclusively technological, which means that we are able to manipulate the physical world ever more sensationally, to increase the speed, the span, and the powers of material existence without any clear idea of what to do with the time gained and the powers acquired. It is to be doubted whether we have produced any persons notably more spiritual than Christ or wiser, in the qualitative sense, than Plato or St. Thomas. We have multiplied books and spread information to an extent unequalled in history, but mere information, mere factual knowledge, is infinitely divisible and may increase by self-analysis without any important growth in quality or actual extent. In short, it has become so pitifully easy to point to the fallacy of modern progress, now that we have seen the atomic bomb and the emergence of Nazism in one of the most cultured nations of Europe, that there should be no need to press the matter further. But the problem contains certain points which the Western mind has such great difficulty in understanding, that we shall have to return to it rather frequently.

## [ii]

It is hardly necessary to say that even in a cosmological and traditional society only a minority of persons understood the principles upon which the social order was grounded. In our own society, too, only a minority understand the scientific procedures so vital to our technology, and only a minority have any real grasp of such widely influential doctrines as those of Freud, Dewey, Einstein or Russell. The influence of the philosopher is out of all relation to physical prowess, and if this is true of philosophers who are no more than theoreticians, who are for the most part teaching mere opinion, a vastly greater influence will be held by an intellectual leadership possessing actual knowledge of principles, as well as theory.[1]

But actual knowledge over and above theory must not be confused with the experimental knowledge of modern science, for, as we saw in the passage from Einstein and Infeld quoted above, scientific knowledge is in fact no more than ingenious guessing. In any event, it has to do with a realm quite other than the universal and eternal wherein lies man's true end—if he has a true end at all. In the modern world neither philosophy, nor science, nor religion have any concept of the kind of knowledge we mean; if it exists at all, they consider it unattainable. Philosophical and scientific knowledge are alike speculative, though the latter is experimentally applicable to the physical world, and religious knowledge is not so much knowledge as belief, which is to say sympathy for certain ideas. It is true that belief is often grounded in a kind of knowledge, the kind known as spiritual or mystical experience. But religious doctrines and ideas—the objects of belief—are quite distinct from mystical experience; they are strictly *analogies* of that experience in rational or symbolic forms.

While modern religion pays little attention to mystical experience, losing itself very largely in the ethical and symbolical analogies of insights long neglected, even mystical knowledge,

---

[1] But even such a leadership as this cannot rescue a society or culture from collapse when it reaches the natural term of its life, any more than the very highest wisdom still preserves the body from old age and death.

as understood in the West, is not always the immediate and universal type of knowledge we have in mind. Mystical knowledge is very frequently coloured by the emotional feelings, not that there is anything *wrong* with such colouring, so long as it is remembered that feelings about the ultimate Reality are just as much analogies as rational ideas. Is it possible, then, to have an immediate non-analogical, knowledge of the universal and eternal? The modern answer, whether philosophical, scientific or religious, is unanimously, 'No', whereas some of our mediaeval predecessors would have answered, with certain reservations, 'Yes'. The same affirmative reply would be given with still less reservation by the spiritual traditions of India and China, for the very basis of their cultures was an immediate knowledge of those universal principles reflected by analogy in the social order, a knowledge enjoyed for centuries by what Toynbee calls a persuasive minority.

We must follow Guénon in using the word 'metaphysic' for this order of knowledge, despite the fact that in modern philosophy as well as in certain religious cults of to-day it means something quite different. Aristotle is supposed to have given the title *Metaphysics* to one of his treatises just because it was written after the *Physics*, but it would be more reasonable to think that the word properly refers to the knowledge of that which is beyond (μετά) the natural order (φύσις)—that is to the universal, infinite, and eternal, as distinct from and beyond the individual, the finite and the temporal.[1]

It is important to distinguish the universal from the general, for this will save endless confusion seeing that the terms are used interchangeably in modern speech. By 'universal' we do not mean any summation or collectivity of all particular things, just as the infinite is not even approached by indefinite summation of the finite, nor eternity by the indefinite extension of time. To say that the ultimate Reality is the universal is *not* to subscribe to the pantheistic proposition that it is the universe, for the universe is, properly speaking, the sum of all finite and individual things. Guénon uses the following scheme to show the difference and the relation between the universal and the general:

---

[1] The word metaphysic is used in the singular to differentiate it from the various *systems* of academic 'metaphysics'.

# INTRODUCTION

Universal

Individual $\left\{\begin{array}{l}\text{General} \\ \\ \text{Particular}^1\end{array}\right.$

Nor must it be imagined, though we shall be going into this in much greater detail, that there is any sort of opposition or incompatibility between the universal and the individual, the infinite and the finite. For the moment it will be enough to remember that the two are 'other' without being 'opposed', somewhat as shape is other than colour but not at all incompatible with it, though this is by no means a perfect analogy. In truth the universal and infinite has no opposite at all because it is absolutely all-inclusive.

From the standpoint of traditional cultures, knowledge of the universal and infinite is man's true end. A little self-analysis should be enough to show that this is in fact what every man desires, whether he is aware of it or not. In most men this desire is only known by analogy in terms of his rational and emotional hunger. As a rational being he is infinitely curious, and as an emotional being he yearns for infinite joy and love; thus he is never content with the attainment of finite goals. In the religious language of St. Augustine, God has put salt in our mouths so that we shall thirst for him. But rational and emotional hunger can never of themselves attain the infinite, any more than the indefinite addition of numbers can attain it. Reason and emotion hunger for more and more, and the indefinite 'more and more' is merely the best temporal and spatial analogy of the infinite. This is why theology sets the vision of God beyond the powers of reason and feeling, stating that as a finite being man can only know God directly by means of a special grace termed the *lumen gloriae*. In the language of metaphysic this *lumen gloriae* is a knowledge of the infinite superior to rational or emotional knowledge, a knowledge which reason and emotion are, however, able to enjoy in some analogical form suited to their natures.

The realization of metaphysical knowledge will therefore depend on the presence in man of some higher faculty than reason

[1] This is a simplification of the scheme used on p. 33 of his *Man and His Becoming* (London, 1945). He makes a further distinction between the general and the collective, adding the collective and the singular as sub-classes of the particular, but this need not detain us here.

or feeling. This faculty is properly called the *intellect*, though the meaning of this word has been degraded in the same way as the word 'metaphysics'. As in modern philosophy metaphysics is speculation and theorization about ultimates without the least degree of immediate knowledge or realization, so the intellect has come to be identified with the logical and speculative faculty of reason. But reason is the faculty which generalizes from particulars; it belongs solely to the individual order, and thus has no point of contact with the universal. On the other hand, the intellect while present in man is not of man; it belongs to the universal and not the individual order.

As in scholastic theology the *lumen gloriae* has a given character, which is why it is called a grace, so in metaphysic there is a corresponding 'givenness' in intellectual knowledge. That is to say, knowledge of the universal is not something to be attained or approached by stages and methods. Stages, methods and processes belong to reason, feeling and sensation, but just as one cannot reach the sky by climbing, so the metaphysical infinity is not attainable through degrees of analogical knowledge. This is why it is always more exact to say that intellectual knowledge is realized rather than attained, because the word 'realization' implies the discovery of something already present or given. The sky appears to be above us, but in fact we live in its midst.

Theology offers another parallel to metaphysic in saying that the *lumen gloriae* is never vouchsafed to man until the life beyond death, though when this is transposed into metaphysical language, death will refer to something quite other than bodily demise. Metaphysically, the division between 'this' life and the eternal life beyond death is precisely the division between the individual and the universal, between sensation, feeling and reason on the one hand and intellect on the other. Theology as a strictly analogical science speaks of the eternal in terms of time, as something *after* death. But in metaphysic the word 'after' can have no relation to eternity which, being timeless, is present at every point of time.

The foregoing should be enough to show how foreign a true metaphysic is to the modern Western mind, how current philosophy, science and religion offer nothing actually equivalent to it, and how this fact explains their present confused state. For if religious knowledge in particular is an analogy of universal knowledge, how can it be anything but confused if the knowledge which it is supposed to represent by analogy is absent or unrealized?

Neither believers nor unbelievers seem to be aware of the analogical nature of religion. Every analogy breaks down when pressed beyond its proper limits, and the difficulty which the modern mind experiences in accepting Catholic Christianity as a doctrine is very largely due to the fact that it has been expected to explain things which it cannot explain, and has been found inconsistent when pursued beyond certain bounds. For example, as soon as it is seen that the ultimate Reality is eternal rather than everlasting, there arises the impossible problem of relating, *within a single framework of thought*, a strictly eternal God to a religion so essentially historical as Christianity. If God is timeless, how can he be said to take different attitudes to, or perform different operations on, the soul before and after Baptism? If he is truly infinite and universally active, how can he be said to be more incarnate in Jesus than in anyone else?

More important still, if God is both omnipotent and eternal in the metaphysical sense, how can he not be responsible for the origin of evil?

Questions such as these, to name but a few, are never satisfactorily answered in religion's own terms. The theologians either retreat into the realm of 'necessary mystery', or offer very tortuous solutions which are unintelligible to the ordinary man and illogical to the philosopher. Present-day religion is unable to fall back upon any metaphysical certainty to which it can refer its doctrines as *analogically* valid. The most serious result of this fact is not so much that multitudes of ordinary folk find it hard to believe in Christianity, but that clergy and theologians themselves are bedevilled with doubts which they are loath to admit even to themselves. The result of such repressed doubts is that the leaders of religion do not speak with conviction, a fact which even the most impressive outward show of authority fails to conceal. This does not mean that they are wilfully insincere. They want to believe; they know that social salvation depends on the acceptance of what they have to say; therefore they dismiss the rankling doubt as a temptation rather than an actual state of the soul. But the light of real conviction does not shine, or, save in very rare circumstances, shines in such a way as to make it suspect of fanaticism or philosophical immaturity.

It is true that there is a movement among 'disillusioned intellectuals' to return to Catholic doctrine, but more than often this is only the result of a very understandable fear of confusion which makes men run for safety to the most impressive authority available. All this is, indeed, something in the right direction simply because religion is our nearest approach to metaphysic, but without the basis of metaphysical certainty it is a castle without foundation. Such certainty is not beyond reach, though, as will appear in due course, it is not found without willingness to take the very greatest risks.

Two difficulties stand in the way of the modern mind accepting anything of this nature. The first is that the average occidental cannot see how a knowledge of the infinite can produce any significant result, or how it can even be called knowledge. For all practical purposes he can see no distinction between infinity and nothing, for which reason knowledge of the infinite would seem the same as no knowledge at all—mere unconsciousness or emptiness of mind. The second is that his contacts with any existing source of this knowledge are, if known to him at all, purely second-hand—through books about mediaeval or oriental 'mysticism' usually written by cranks or by well-meaning but wholly puzzled academicians. Therefore, having never come across such knowledge himself, he is inclined to dismiss the entire subject as dreams and self-delusion.

From the standpoint of reason, feeling, or sensation the infinite is necessarily incomprehensible. It seems like nothing just as colour must seem like nothing to one congenitally blind. As beauty of colour might be suggested to a blind man by the analogy of music, so the infinite is suggested to reason and feeling by the idea of God the Creator and Lover of the universe, since the infinite 'produces' and embraces the finite. Negative terms are used of the ultimate Reality simply because it has none of the dimensions of the individual and finite realm, as one might say of colour that it is neither long nor short, high nor low, round nor square, rough nor smooth.

Perhaps the best way of suggesting the potency of the infinite is through the analogy of our own consciousness. Pure, essential awareness—that mysterious field in each one of us which *knows*—is not describable in terms of anything known. Like a light shining upon a variety of objects, it would be invisible if the objects were not there to reflect it. The light shows us things large and small, white and black, long and short. But in itself the light, or our field of consciousness, is neither large nor small, nor any other of the qualities, forms, and objects which it reveals. Yet if the light were not present, none of the objects would be revealed. Similarly, the infinite may be considered not only as that which illumines and knows the universe, but also as that which, by the same act, generates the things known. As light reveals squareness but is not squareness, so the infinite generates, and yet is not, the finite. However, we shall see that such words as 'produce' and 'generate' can only be used of the infinite analogically, and on condition that they involve no idea of effort or lapse of time in the creative act.

Contrary to widespread belief, the knowledge and contemplation of the infinite is not a state of trance, for because of the truth that there is no opposition between the infinite and the finite, knowledge of the infinite may be compatible with all possible states of mind, feeling and sensation. Intellectual knowledge is an inclusive, not an exclusive, state of consciousness. Thus one of the important principles of scholastic theology was that the supernatural (i.e. the metaphysical) does not obliterate nature but perfects it. Similarly, knowledge of the infinite does not obliterate ordinary knowledge; on the contrary, it perfects it just as formless light reveals the clarity of forms. According to the same principle, the person who realizes this knowledge is in no way bound to exclude himself hermit-wise from ordinary life; indeed, he is if anything more free than the average man to enter into that life, and to devote himself in the most unreserved way to any work or activity that may be appropriate.

Trance states of consciousness, and more especially those described as ecstasy or rapture, belong more properly to mysticism than to metaphysic because they are primarily states of feeling and, as such, exclude other states of feeling just as sorrow excludes merriment. In other words, mystical ecstasy is simply an analogy of intellectual knowledge in terms of feeling, and is in no way essential to metaphysical realization.

The principal circumstance which makes the Western mind suspect this kind of knowledge is that the cultures which value it do not 'show results' in terms of sensationally productive busyness. They do not use their knowledge to perfect the quantitative manufacture of food, clothes, automobiles, vitamin pills, refrigerators and baths. But the modern mind finds it tremendously hard to understand that people who, for reasons of faith or knowledge, are not particularly afraid of pain, discomfort or death, simply cannot share this exaggerated concern for physical well-being. When you know that life is eternal, you will be in no hurry to crowd as many sensations as possible into seventy years, and as a result you will appreciate sensations more keenly. It is absurd to suppose that, apart from certain aberrations, the oriental and medieval cultures *despise* physical life; men who wrote the *Kama Sutra*, [1] made Chinese pottery, and built Gothic cathedrals should least of all be accused of contempt of material. On the other hand, the builders of Westside Chicago and East London, of Madison Square Garden and King's Cross Station, could hardly be accused of any excessive reverence for material.

In comparing cultures, however, it is always fatally easy to set the best of one against the worst of the other, and we do not deny that in traditional societies there may be found slums, filth, disease, cruelty, and tyranny. These have always been the lot of man, especially in densely populated areas, because there have always been dirty, cruel, and domineering people. It is impossible, and it would be most ungracious, to deny the very real benefits which Western science, and especially medicine, have bestowed on the human race, even though this often involves the dangerous procedure of tinkering with an organism which we do not fully understand. It is likewise impossible to idealize the Orient *in toto*, and to overlook the filth, disease, and poverty in which so many millions of its peoples have lived.

While it is true that man cannot live by bread alone, it is also true that he cannot live without bread. Bread is essential for human life, but relation to man's spiritual end is also essential. The Western mind is in little danger of neglecting the necessity of bread. But it is in such total forgetfulness of man's spiritual end, that to put this necessity *on the same level* as the need for bread would be to give it far too little emphasis. We must learn to see a hierarchy of truths, to see that of the many things which are *necessary*, some are of a higher order than others. While observing that the physical body cannot live without kidneys, we must not overlook the fact that still less can it live without the heart. It is true that millions need bread most urgently. But they need something else *at the same time*—not later, not when we 'get around to it' after the bread has been supplied. For to give

[1] The official Hindu doctrines on the art of marital love.

bread alone, to try to heal the physical ill *before* the spiritual, is merely to endanger mankind with the confusion of still more unintegrated and meaningless lives with power to pursue aimless and clashing courses. Perhaps there are occasions when bread simply has to come first in point of time. One must by no means undervalue the compassionate urgency of those who labour almost exclusively for the relief of pain and starvation. But without spiritual life this labour can no more continue than man can work without rest. If Christ himself withdrew into the mountains to pray, the most ardent 'muscular Christian' cannot use the world's urgent need for bread as an excuse for the indefinite postponement of spiritual contemplation. Yet in most Christian churches the average sermon is a stirring call to action directed to people who, having no spiritual repose, are not ready to be spiritually awake. It is essential, therefore, that while we give alms to oriental poverty, we help ourselves to oriental wisdom, lacking which, we shall shortly have no alms to give.

We may have to face the tragedy that the whole situation of modern man is so far out of hand that we shall be compelled to let external events take their terrible course. In this case the only hope left will be the withdrawal of a remnant into a temporary solitude of the spirit, there to derive power from the only source which can *in the long run* change human life for the better. Traditional cultures maintain that human character changes from the inside outwards, and that the external way of life results wholly from internal causes. Changes of personality which follow this direction are extremely slow but sure. On the other hand, reforms of man's external life by purely technological and legislative means put the unregenerate 'inner man' in possession of vast powers which are just as easily used for destruction as for creation. Furthermore, their sensational character diverts his entire attention to the external side of life which, because it is the circumference rather than the centre of being, is the area of maximum disunity. Hence the rapid disintegration of a purely external and technological society.

But the point of this comparison is not to propose any romantic notion of 'returning to the good old days', or to judge modern Western society as nothing more than a bad mistake which should never have happened. On the contrary, it is possible that the modern experiment in the control of external nature, its brilliant success in one direction and its tragic failure in another, may serve more than any other event in human history to make men consider their true end on a scale never attained in the ancient world. The temptation to live merely as a highly complex animal and to treat the physical world as the ultimate reality and true end of life has always been present for millions of souls who lacked the means to try it. It may be hoped that this magnificent trial and failure, which has affected not the West alone but the whole world, was necessary to get the temptation out of the human system, at least in some degree.

For those who enjoy metaphysical knowledge the physical world has an importance of a very different kind, resembling the importance of his medium to an artist. The material is used, not served, and is valued, not as the supremely desirable good, but as one of many means of expression for the 'play' of the infinite. Intrinsically, material life offers no obstruction whatsoever to the realization of man's true end, and is only regarded as something to be shunned in certain special circumstances (more prevalent at some times than at others) where the flesh has been given an excessive value.[1]

If the foregoing may have helped to show that knowledge of the infinite is quite other than mere empty-mindedness, there remains the final problem of whether such knowledge exists at all. This problem must actually be reduced to another: upon what grounds will the modern mind believe that *anything* exists? Certainly not solely on those of immediate experience, for modern man believes in all kinds of things which he has never sensed nor even clearly understood. On the strictly second-hand testimony of scientists he believes that the earth revolves around the sun, that matter is composed of electrons (which not even scientists have actually seen), that light follows a curved path in space, and that man has evolved from apes. Most of this he believes on pure faith in the scientists' good judgment and unanimity. The scientists themselves believe it on pure faith in the reliability of their minds, senses and instruments. The truth of such beliefs is made somewhat more impressive by the fact that some of them have practical applications. There is even a practical application for a concept so abstract as the square root

[1] This is the reason for the pronounced asceticism of Christianity in the Graeco-Roman world, despite the fact that the central Christian dogma is the union of God with the flesh in Christ.

of minus one, though even a mathematician cannot actually visualize it.

There is at least this much evidence for the reality of metaphysical knowledge. Witnesses to its existence have lived and taught since the beginning of known history, and if truthfulness and reliability have any connection with moral integrity, these witnesses have the best possible credentials. Furthermore, the witnesses to this knowledge present a much more surprising unanimity than the scientists because they have lived in such widely distant times and places that in countless instances there has been no possibility of their influencing and persuading one another.

Metaphysicians of the Christian tradition—pseudo-Dionysius, Eckhart, Albert the Great—teach essentially the same doctrine as Shankara and the Upanishads, and they in their turn the same as Chinese Taoism and the Sufis of Islam. Add to this the corroborative support of the thousands who are more strictly mystics, and we have the most impressively unanimous body of teaching in the whole world. Of course there are variations depending on cultural background, but these hardly touch the essentials in spite of what has been said by 'interested' propagandists. The attempts which have been made to show that mystics of the Christian tradition represent a true knowledge as against the 'false mysticism' of the Hindus, Buddhists and Taoists quite invariably reveal that the latter have been seriously misunderstood. This misunderstanding is instantly shown by the use of such words as 'pantheism', 'monism', and 'nihilism' in connection with the Eastern doctrines, words denoting Western conceptions which have no relation whatsoever to metaphysical knowledge. Similarly, it is an absolute begging of the question to distinguish Christian from other doctrines on the ground that the former is supernatural and revealed, and the latter merely natural. *All* the doctrines in question claim a supernatural and revealed character. Such judgments as these are prejudice pure and simple, because they rest on the foregone conclusion that a Christian doctrine *must* be superior to any other kind of doctrine, whether known or unknown, past or future, actual or potential.[1]

[1] Cf. St. Ambrose on 1 Corinthians xii. 3: 'All that is true, by whomsoever it has been said, is from the Holy Spirit.' Lest the above statements give offence to our Christian brethren who think this way

Unhappily it is still the opinion of many orientalists that the doctrines of Hinduism and Buddhism, for example, are radically incompatible, and that therefore this unity of metaphysical doctrine does not exist even in Asia. While it is true that ignorant adherents of these teachings indulge in sectarian rivalries, as in the West, the most reliable scholarship of to-day concurs with the more enlightened Hindus and Buddhists in finding no *essential* conflicts at all. There can be no question that the core of Hinduism, Buddhism, and Taoism is one *sanātana dharma*, one universal and common realization whose only differences are adaptations to external circumstances.[1]

In none of the instances mentioned is metaphysical knowledge regarded as simple theory, but rather as the most immediate kind of experience. On the other hand, many things termed 'scientific facts' are actually theories based on sensual stimuli, as Einstein and Infeld explain, and whereas 'scientific facts' have shown a remarkable tendency to change within a mere two centuries, metaphysical doctrines have remained essentially the same throughout history.

It is not hard to imagine the sort of argument that might be advanced against this point of view. For untold centuries, it will be said, human beings including those of the most upright character believed on the unanimous and immediate evidence

in perfectly good faith, we ask their patience until the next chapter, where the true distinction between Christian and other types of doctrine will be fully considered. It will be shown that the Western mind is mistaken in regarding the chief oriental doctrines as religious and therefore in any way opposed to Christianity.

[1] For example, the academic and the popular Western notion that the Buddha denied the Brahmanic doctrine of the eternal and supra-individual Self (*atma*) in man is simply absurd in view of the many texts in the Pali scriptures which precisely teach this doctrine. 'Be such as have the Self (Pali, *atta*) as your lamp, Self as only refuge. *Atta-dipa viharatha atta-sarana.*' (*Digha Nikaya*, ii. 101.) The Buddha's doctrine of 'no-self' (*anatta*) is simply the denial that the Self is individual, that it belongs in any way to particular human beings. In view of this the familiar translation of the above passage as 'Be ye lamps unto yourselves, be ye a refuge unto yourselves' makes no sense at all. See the admirable discussion of this whole matter in Coomaraswamy's *Hinduism and Buddhism* (New York, 1943), and the corroborative evidence in C. A. F. Rhys-David's *Outlines of Buddhism* (London, 1934), and *What Was the Original Gospel in Buddhism?* (London, 1938). See also Northrop's *Meeting of East and West* (New York, 1946), pp. 312-74.

of their senses that the sun revolved round the earth, that matter was solid through and through, that diseases were the result of fluids called humours, and that the moon was larger than Venus. The moral—prejudice dies hard, and seeing is not always believing.

The answer is that we are not discussing ideas based on the evidence of the senses, evidence which the metaphysicians have always described as the most relative kind of knowledge. Indeed, so far as the relativism of the physical universe is concerned, metaphysical doctrines are in principal agreement with Einstein. Because of the omnipresence of the infinite, any point in the universe may be regarded as central—which is not far from the astronomical application of relativity, namely, that in a universe where all motion is relative any point may arbitrarily be selected as the centre of the whole.

Whereas sense knowledge is mediate, intellectual knowledge is immediate; no gap of any kind exists between the knowing subject and the known object. Though this will require much further explanation at the proper point, the metaphysical knowledge of the infinite is as irreducible and as certain as the simple knowledge of existence—that something or other *is*. Nothing, from the standpoint of ordinary experience, is more certain than that there is such a thing as existence, however unknown in essence. It is, of course, possible to postulate the doubt that 'there is not', because it is possible to postulate absolutely anything, such as a finite plane triangle the summation of whose angles is two hundred and ten degrees, or a square circle. But to say that the knowledge of existence is not perfectly certain knowledge because it is possible to postulate that nothing exists is to play with mere words in the most absurd manner imaginable. To say that anything can be doubted is only to say that words can be strung together in any order; the word 'nothing' can be written in front of the word 'exists' to form a sentence, but to imagine that this can constitute a serious doubt or even a serious concept is to be the most ridiculous victim of mere verbalism. We shall have to say then that the knowledge of being is certain and irreducible knowledge, and because, as will be shown, metaphysical knowledge is of the same wholly immediate order, it is impossible for one who experiences it to entertain the slightest doubt of its truth.

# I. THE INFINITE AND THE FINITE

## OUTLINE

1. Knowledge of the infinite Reality is immediate, and cannot be approached through deduction and logic.

Metaphysical knowledge and doctrine, as we find it in the Vedanta and other oriental teachings, is quite distinct from religious knowledge, but not at all in conflict with it. As religion begins with revelation, metaphysical knowledge begins with actual realization, which is the basis of all that follows.

2. The meaning of *infinite*. The sizeless and spaceless rather than the indefinitely vast. The eternal is timeless rather than everlasting. The infinite corresponds to the ground of man's consciousness, which, though not an object, though sizeless and formless, embraces all forms and objects.

The religious idea of God is an analogy of the infinite in finite terms, i.e. in positive, concrete and objective ideas. But these terms cannot be used in the same framework of thought as the negative terms of metaphysic without hopeless confusion.

3. Because the infinite is *not opposed* to the finite, being all-inclusive, there is no real problem of creation, i.e. of *how* it is possible for the infinite to produce the finite. The infinite includes the possibility of the finite world in principle and by definition. It produces things by becoming finite, without ceasing to be its infinite Self. Yet it is not the One as opposed to the Many, but includes both unity and multiplicity.

The religious idea of God cannot do full duty for the metaphysical infinity. For God is One, and to say that the universe is a self-limitation of God is to say that all things are one. This is a monism or pantheism which excludes the reality and significance of finite things. But the infinite *includes* the finite in a unity (or non-duality) which does not obliterate distinctions.

# I. THE INFINITE AND THE FINITE

## [i]

There is no point from which knowledge of the infinite can begin, other than the infinite itself. From the start, we are in the disconcerting position of setting out to understand something which has no beginning, which cannot be approached from any ordinary, finite point of reference. This is perhaps inconvenient and confusing, but the truth remains that one cannot work up to the subject of metaphysic by easy stages. A million to the power of a million is no nearer to infinity than one. Like the Chinese sage Lao-tzu, metaphysic is born fully aged; it comes from the womb an old man with long white whiskers. It has no history, no development. Its earliest known written records are as advanced as its most recent, and all of them plunge straight into the heart of their subject without apologies or preliminaries.

'In the heart of all things, of whatever there is in the universe, dwells the Lord. He alone is the reality. Wherefore, renouncing vain appearances, rejoice in him.'[1]

'The Tao that can be expressed is not the eternal Tao; the name that can be defined is not the unchanging name.'[2]

'OM. This eternal Word is all: what was, what is and what shall be, and what beyond is in eternity. All is OM.'[3]

'In the beginning was the Word, and the Word was with God, and the Word was God. . . . All things were made through him, and without him was not anything made that was made.'[4]

Almost without exception the sacred writings begin their exposition of the ultimate Reality without preface, argument or proof. The modern philosopher will regard this as hopeless prejudice, for to adopt the existence of the infinite or of God as

[1] *Isha Upanishad*. From *The Upanishads*, trs. Prabhavananda and Manchester (Hollywood, 1947).
[2] *Tao Te Ching*, i. trs. Ch'u Ta-kao (London, 1937).
[3] *Mandukya Upanishad*. From *Himalayas of the Soul*, trs. Juan Mascaro (London, 1938).
[4] St. John i.

one's major premise is against every rule of his science. But it cannot be otherwise, for as the reality of light cannot be proved or described in terms of visible shape, the reality of the infinite cannot be proved in terms of the finite. For this reason every attempt to prove the existence of God by logic is a foregone failure. Logic cannot reach God. It may travel backwards in time from effect to cause, effect to cause, but as long as it stays in time, as it must, it cannot touch the eternal. That which does not begin with the infinite cannot end with it. The most that can be said is that finite contingencies suggest the infinite; in no sense can they be said to prove it. The stream of existence seems to run from the infinite to the finite so that one cannot swim against it. For purposes of discussion one can reach the infinite only by jumping upstream like a salmon, though for purposes of realization, of true knowledge, it will be seen that, flow as far as it may, the stream can never leave the infinite.

There is a parallel to this in ordinary experience. All philosophy, all everyday knowledge, must begin from oneself; it must assume a knower as the given and irreducible basis of knowledge. But no amount of knowledge proves the existence of a knower, for the simple reason that the knower cannot be the object of its own knowledge. By proof the philosopher means objective proof, and if the knower can never be its own object, it can never be objectively proved. Objective knowledge only suggests a knower as the finite only suggests the infinite. And as the infinite cannot be described in terms of anything finite, and is therefore described negatively as the unlimited Reality, the knower cannot be described in terms of anything known. The conscious Self cannot be called long or short, large or small, black or white, pleasant or painful, for it transcends the various objects of its knowledge as the infinite transcends the finite. But as the infinite is the ground of the finite, the knower is the ground of knowledge; apart from the knower, or at least the knowing process, nothing whatsoever would exist from the standpoint of knowledge.

It is therefore quite idle to entertain any serious doubt as to the reality of the knower, because the knower can no more become its own object of knowledge than a finger can catch hold of itself. The very notion of the Self having an objective knowledge of itself is actually quite meaningless—one of those concepts which come into being as the result of playing with words.

From the viewpoint of metaphysic, *objective* knowledge of the Self is not only impossible but unnecessary. Properly understood, the Self is like light, which has no need to illumine itself because it is already luminous.

We shall see that in metaphysic there is the closest connection, something much more than mere analogical resemblance, between the Self, as the irreducible ground of knowledge, and the infinite. Speaking of the knowledge proper to the infinite as the total knower of the universe, Shankara says:

'Now a distinct and definite knowledge is possible in respect of everything capable of becoming an object of knowledge: but it is not possible in the case of That which cannot become such an object. That is *Brahma*, for It is the Knower, and the Knower can know other things, but cannot make Itself the object of Its own knowledge, in the same way that fire can burn other things but cannot burn itself. Neither can it be said that *Brahma* is able to become an object of knowledge for anything other than Itself, since outside Itself there is nothing which can possess knowledge.'[1]

There is no possessor of knowledge other than *Brahma* because all knowledge whatsoever is a participation in infinite knowledge, and the infinite has no more need to know itself as an object than fire to burn itself.

Setting aside the question of the true relationship between the infinite and the Self, it should now be clear why philosophy and metaphysic alike must begin from an irreducible ground. The philosopher may call this ground an assumption or postulate, but, even in his own case, it is nothing quite so theoretical. The philosopher's intuitive and subjective knowledge of his own existence as a knower may not be objective and proven knowledge, but in actuality it is something much better, though the manner of thinking peculiar to modern philosophy does not permit its recognition. Objective and scientific knowledge is mediate and relative, but the subjective knowledge of the Self is immediate, and thus as absolute and certain as anything in the realm of philosophy can be. Yet it cannot be an object of logical proof. Indeed, objective knowledge is only verifiable as probable, never as certain.

For metaphysic likewise the infinite is the irreducible ground

[1] Commentary on *Kena Upanishad*. Quoted in Guénon, *Man and His Becoming According to the Vedanta* (London, 1945), p. 114.

of all knowledge, and is known immediately as distinct from objectively. As the ground of all beings it is as free from the limitations and determinations of beings as the knower from those of the things known. Since both proof and doubt can have reference only to known objects, the infinite is accessible to neither. As ultimate and infinite Reality there is no external standpoint from which to doubt it or prove it. We are compelled, then, to take it as given.

Yet there is this obvious objection: we all have the intuitive and subjective knowledge of our own existence, and are therefore quite prepared to call it certain and irreducible; but we do not seem to have the same kind of knowledge of the ultimate Reality. How then can we accept it as our starting point? The answer is that in principle the two are the same, all knowledge being a participation in the infinite knowledge, but that for purposes of 'generating' the finite world the ultimate Reality has, as it were, the power of restricting its own knowledge, of becoming finite. This paradox will be clarified when the time comes to show that the infinite and the finite are neither opposed nor mutually exclusive.

Because the nearest approximation to metaphysic in the Western world of to-day is religion, it will be necessary, as we describe the metaphysical doctrines, to transpose them also into their religious equivalents. This is the more important because of the supposed conflict between a metaphysic such as the Vedanta and a religion such as Catholicism—a conflict which is in truth as absurd and impossible as between music and the dance. It is indeed natural for the average occidental to think that all doctrines about the ultimate Reality and the true end of man's life are religious in the same sense as his own. But this assumption is incorrect, and is the cause of much wholly unnecessary controversy and ill feeling. Let it be said here, then, that necessary as the metaphysical viewpoint may be to the Western world, there is not the slightest conflict between it and the fullest and most traditional Catholic orthodoxy. If any objections to such orthodoxy exist, they must be adduced on religious and not on metaphysical grounds. There is, therefore, absolutely nothing of a metaphysical nature to prevent anyone from accepting the traditional Christian doctrines without reservation or alteration.

The reason for this absence of conflict is that, as already indicated, the religious mode of knowledge is mediate, objective and analogical, and does not claim to be anything else. On the other hand, metaphysical knowledge is immediate, being in the sphere of the intellect (or the Self), whereas religion is a knowledge of the infinite in terms of reason, feeling, and sense. In religion the formless and imageless ultimate Reality is translated into finite images, somewhat as magnetic lines of force are clothed with iron filings for experimental observation. These images are of three kinds:

1. Rational images or ideas. These are forms seen in the mind's eye, which is the strict meaning of the word 'idea', and forms of this kind make up the main body of religious doctrine. Metaphysical doctrines are not ideas in this sense, for the mind is incapable of forming any image of the eternal, if the word be used in its true meaning. The mind can conceive the eternal as everlasting time, but this is analogy pure and simple. It can only think about the truly eternal negatively. A window, for example, cannot be described in terms of bricks; it is outlined by bricks, but does not consist of them. Similarly, for purposes of metaphysical doctrine, the infinite is 'outlined' by the limitations of time and space, but the outline cannot be filled in in terms of thought.

2. Feeling images or values. In order to relate the infinite to man's feeling nature, it must be clothed in some emotionally moving analogy. Such a 'non-idea' as the Eternal or the Absolute cannot have the feeling value which is attached to ideas such as God, the Everlasting Father, the Divine Love, or the King of Glory—ideas which have none the less a perfectly real correspondence to their infinite original.

3. Sense images or sacraments. For the original apostles, Christ Himself would come, at least in part, under this category, being the Eternal Word made flesh. To Christians of later times the Incarnate Word is sensed indirectly in the sacraments, in the physical worship of the Church, and in the record of the Gospels.

In creed, in code (the realm of values), and in cult religion constitutes a marvellous incarnation or external projection of the ultimate Reality, so expressed as to be meaningful and effective for every level of man's nature. This process is seen at its best in Christianity, whose very essence is the knowledge of the Absolute in Christ, who, in his human nature, is the 'express image' of the Father. He is the analogy *par excellence*, for in the historical character of Jesus there is a more perfect idea of God than can be expressed in any amount of rational concepts.[1]

The peculiar significance of the *historicity* of Christ as the God-man cannot be properly discussed until we have been through the main principles of metaphysical doctrine. But at this stage the orthodox Christian may object that if Christ is the supreme source of wisdom on earth, he would surely have taught the metaphysical doctrine if it had been of such vital importance. He cannot relish the thought of going beyond the teaching of Christ for spiritual insights which he did not provide, even though such insights are not strictly religious. Christianity holds that the Church and Scripture contain all things necessary to salvation, and if this be true what is to be gained from any external traditions?

We answer, firstly, that the religious goal of salvation is quite distinct from the metaphysical goal of realization, of knowledge of the infinite Reality. The two are related by analogy, but are not at all the same thing—as we shall show in due course.

Secondly, it must never be forgotten that our knowledge of the teaching of Christ is only that which is handed down by the Church.[2] Now the Church, as such, is not directly concerned

---

[1] Catholic doctrine expresses the analogical and 'projective' character of the knowledge of God through the humanity of Jesus in stating that his divine and human natures are not to be confused. His manhood is not his Godhead; yet because the man Jesus is united to the Person of God the Son, his character as man is a perfect expression of the divine nature in strictly human terms. In speaking of the Incarnation, or of other religious forms, as 'projections', we are not using the word in a merely psychological sense. The sense is that the infinite is 'central' to the finite as the knower to things known, and that religious forms, being finite, are thus projections or extraversions of the interior and infinite centre.

[2] Thus, there is no evidence at all that Jesus did not teach anything of a metaphysical character, or that he considered such matters unimportant. On the contrary, the Fourth Gospel implies metaphysical knowledge because, among other things, it employs the concept of *eternity* in its strict sense. To argue that this Gospel is a late compilation under Greek influence which does not accurately represent the teaching of Jesus, is to discredit the primary source of the Incarnation doctrine. The dogma that Christ is the God-man has no sure foundation in the Synoptic Gospels alone. To argue that Jesus, as a Jew, would have had no 'bent' for metaphysic, is to argue an intellectual defect in the Son of God, to suggest that the divine mind is

with metaphysic. The nature of the Church is sacramental. That is to say, it is a concrete and positive *form* of creed, code and cult, which has its own proper function of representing the spiritual by analogy, and in physical terms. Thus it is quite beyond the design and nature of the Church to employ the negative speech of metaphysical doctrine, or to deal in any way with immediate as distinct from mediate and analogical knowledge.

'The work of the Church in the world is not to teach the mysteries of life, so much as to persuade the soul to that arduous degree of purity at which God Himself becomes her teacher. The work of the Church ends when the knowledge of God begins.'[1]

Having, then, no direct concern with metaphysic, the Church had no concern to hand down, as part of a *religious* tradition, any teaching which Christ might have given of this nature. The Church, its tradition, its teaching, has to do with man as a temporal and historical being; metaphysic has to do with man as an eternal being—not, indeed, with man the individual, but with the Son of Man, the Adam-Kadmon, the Self (*atma*) as distinct from the individual ego (*jiva*).[2]

Religion expresses the metaphysical truth that knowledge of the infinite must begin with the infinite in the idea of revelation. The knowledge of God begins from God, for the prophets precede the theologians. Every attempt to arrive at the idea of God through purely rational and philosophical means is historically later than those prophetic and mystic utterances which gave the philosophers the original idea. In the language of scholastic theology, Faith is consistent with Reason though, by its own power, Reason could never have attained to Faith. The Faith is first revealed, and subsequently the theologian may go to work upon it and show that no principle of Reason is violated in any article of Faith. In like manner, the Church is understood not as a society of men who have come together to find God, but as a society which God has created and called together in order to

strictly limited by Hebrew psychology. But in view of Philo of Alexandria and the Kabbalah, it is hardly accurate to say that Jews have no metaphysical capacity.

[1] Coventry Patmore, *The Rod, the Root, and the Flower* ('Knowledge and Science'), xxii.

[2] On this distinction see below ch. 2, sec. II.

discover himself in men. So, too, the very Incarnation upon which the Church is founded is not the ascent of a man to God, but the descent of God to man. Jesus is considered divine not because he was a man who, by supreme effort, attained the divine state, but because in him 'the Word was made flesh and dwelt among us'.

As religion begins with revelation, metaphysic begins with realization. All that follows, therefore, is the statement of the realization, rather than the speculation, of the metaphysical tradition as it is found in the Vedanta, in Taoism, and its continuation in Mahayana Buddhism, and in the Christian metaphysic which flourished in Graeco-Roman and medieval times until its virtual disappearance in the fifteenth century. No attempt will be made to prove or deduce the metaphysical doctrines step by step from reason or sense experience, since this is impossible. They must first be seen *as a whole*, and then the reader may decide for himself whether, as a whole, they conflict with reason and experience. A picture must be painted fully before it can be understood, since the parts are meaningless without relation to the whole. It is impossible for the artist to justify and explain each stroke of his brush to a bystander as the work goes along. In the end, the picture will speak for itself. Finally, it is always essential to remember that though the language, the theoretical aspect, of metaphysic is not analogical in the same sense as religious language, a certain element of analogy remains so long as there is no immediate realization. The use of analogy is like boiling an egg; if boiled too long it will explode. The important thing is to boil for just long enough—and then eat the egg.

[ii]

Beginning, then, with the infinite, we have to understand as clearly as may be what the word means. Inevitably man's imagination tries to grasp the infinite in terms of size and space, as that which expands outwards forever, or perhaps as that which contracts inwards forever. Similarly, the imagination has to think of the eternal as an unending time series, or perhaps as that ever-diminishing point of time called the moment. If the imagination tries to conceive the infinite in terms of knowledge or consciousness, it must perforce think of an indefinitely vast mass of sentiency, reaching out from its centre to know every detail of the finite universe and beyond. Here, as it were, is a mind without the material or spatial bounds of the five senses. Its sight reaches in all directions; the rocks and stars are transparent, and no conceivable telescope could outdistance the penetration of its vision into interminable space. So, too, in terms of power, imagination pictures the infinite as force multiplied without end to make the simultaneous explosion of every atom in the universe a mere firecracker. But expand, prolong, magnify, and multiply as we may, we are not one fraction nearer to the true infinite than when we began, for the terms of time and space are not applicable to the infinite.

To denote the infinite at all in terms of thought we shall have to 'outline' it by the limitations of space and time, calling it the sizeless or spaceless and the timeless. We shall have to try to think of the infinite as having no size at all, so that, regarding it from the standpoint of space, we shall be able to say that the infinite exists in its entirety at every point of space. Or, to put it in another way, from the standpoint of the infinite every point of space is absolutely *here*, for there is not a different infinite at every place. In yet another way, we can say that there is no space or distance between the whole infinite and anything at all.

The eternal or timeless must be understood in the same way. Eternity is immediately present at every moment of time, or, from the standpoint of eternity, every moment of time, past, present, or future, is absolutely *now*. At a given moment of time several separate points in space, such as the five fingers, may be seen at once. So from the one 'moment' of eternity, the eternal Now, all separate points of time are simultaneously present.

The accompanying diagram may help to clarify this concept. The circle represents time and space; the centre point, O, represents the infinite and eternal. From the point A, an event in time and space, the events B and C are respectively nearer and farther away. In the time-series, B is before A, and C is after A. But A, B, and C are all equidistant from O. The radii AO, BO, and CO represent a relation of immediate presence in space and time alike, and must be imagined as having no spatial or temporal length. At this the entire diagram will disappear, having, it is hoped, served its purpose.

The same modifications must be made to the imagination's picture of the infinite as the Knower of the universe, as infinite consciousness or omniscience. In reality there can be no possibility of the infinite consciousness knowing things at a distance. Just as every point of time and space is, to the infinite, absolutely here and now, so it knows everything as immediately present to its entire Self, without, however, abolishing the distances and the times between the things known.

There is an interesting similarity to this in our own consciousness, though with one important difference. Everything that we know is known in our minds. If we have an impression of a tree ten feet away, the impressions both of the tree and of the ten feet are *in* our consciousness, which does not itself occupy any space or have any size. The tree as an object of knowledge, as well as the space between the tree and our bodies, is immediately

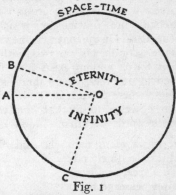

Fig. 1

present to our consciousness, although this does not abolish the distance between our bodies and the tree. The important difference, however, is this, that our consciousness, though spaceless, is limited by space; we know nothing of what is a hundred miles from the tree. And though our consciousness is timeless, because for pure consciousness time is always *now* and even memories are a *present* experience, it is limited by time; it can focus its attention only on one thing at a time. This paradox will be explained when we come to consider the possibility of the self-limitation of the infinite, but for the moment the point is simply that things can be at once immediately present to consciousness and distant from each other.

In sum, then, omniscience must mean that the infinite knows every single object simultaneously. It will, furthermore, know each object with its entire Self, as if each object were the one and only thing to be known. Because our consciousness can attend to only one thing at a time, such a state of affairs is as far beyond imagination as anything could be.

Now it may seem strange to speak of the infinite as conscious, as a knowing subject. The modern mind suffers from the odd prejudice that consciousness is a purely superficial outgrowth of reality, and that the more fundamental a power, principle or substance becomes, the more blind and unconscious it must be. Others imagine that consciousness is a determination, a finite quality, and therefore inapplicable to the infinite. It is true that consciousness *as we know it* is to a degree finite and determined. But as infinite *being* is the necessary ground of finite existence, infinite consciousness is the necessary ground of finite knowledge and experience. Pure consciousness is no more a determination than being itself. On the contrary, the two are identical and no determinations, or objects, can exist without them.[1]

It is obvious that, for us, nothing exists apart from consciousness. For all practical purposes, where there is no experience there are no things; where there is no knowledge there is no reality. This is not, however, to say that what we do not know does not exist. In the words of a famous limerick

> 'There was a young man who said: "God,
> I find it exceedingly odd
>     That a tree, as a tree,
>     Simply ceases to be
> When there's no one around in the quad."
>
> "Young man, your astonishment's odd;
> I am always about in the quad.
>     So the tree, as a tree,
>     Continues to be
> Since observed by yours faithfully God." '

[1] Various oriental texts speak of the infinite as 'neither conscious nor unconscious, neither being nor non-being'. The reference is, of course, to *finite* consciousness and being which exist in opposition to unconsciousness and nothingness. Pure or absolute unconsciousness and non-being are mere verbalisms. One cannot have absolute non-existence! The term can only be used relatively, as when we say that a given finite object does not exist. There is the existence and non-existence, the consciousness and unconsciousness of finite objects. But there is no absolute non-being or unconsciousness standing over against the *necessary* being and consciousness of the infinite.

Things are things, objects are objects, only because they participate in the infinite being and consciousness. Were the infinite unconscious, consciousness would have emerged *ex nihilo* in a manner far more contradictory than a fig growing from a thistle. If all things are merely special forms of a primal blind force or substance, consciousness is nothing but a special form of unconsciousness—which is as absurd as saying that heat is a special form of cold, or that energy is a particular mode of inertia.

The notion that the ultimate Reality must be less conscious than man is one of the most striking examples of the confusion of the temporal with the eternal. For the idea comes from the observation that things which precede man in time are less conscious and, going back earlier, unconscious. But the supposition that things are fully explainable by what precedes them in time, and that what is earliest in time is closest to the nature of eternity is pure imagination. Things may to some degree be explained by their history, but no amount of history will explain why or how there happens to be any history at all. A principle which will bear considerable thought is that the attempt to explain the present by the past alone is virtually an attempt to derive what exists from what does not. As a *sufficient* cause of the present, the past has the peculiar disqualification of not existing.

Many of the terms for the infinite employed in the various metaphysical traditions signify nothing so much as pure consciousness—the Self, the Light, Universal Mind (*alaya-vijnana*), and even the Void (*sunyata*), which in Mahayana Buddhism denotes not so much mere emptiness as an absolute clarity and transparency. The truth, however, that the infinite is conscious is, like its very existence, beyond any objective proof. It comes from the metaphysical realization that man's consciousness, which is the necessary ground of his experience, is a particular mode of the ultimate Reality and is, in essence, identical with the ground of the whole universe. That which lies at the foundation of the universe will be immeasurably *more*—not less— than that which underlies human experience.

As regards infinite power, or omnipotence, the infinite must not be thought of as indefinitely magnified force or energy, whether actual or potential.[1] The infinite acts without effort;

[1] 'That which of itself must necessarily be, can nowise be possibly, since what of itself must be necessarily has no cause, whereas whatever can be possibly, has a cause. Now God, in himself, must

57

without the use of energy, it produces energy, just as it produces the finite without being finite itself, in its own essence. In this way it may produce any amount of finite energy, energy itself being a finite thing like time and space. To put it in another way, the infinite moves things without either moving or being moved itself.

'Tao is ever inactive, and yet there is nothing that it does not do.'[1]

'The Spirit, without moving, is swifter than the mind; the senses cannot reach him: he is ever beyond them. Standing still, he overtakes those who run.'[2]

Because of its omnipresence at every point of time and space, it will follow also that the infinite does not act upon anything at a distance, which is why its action does not require that it move. To act at a distance is to cause something to move by pushing it away or pulling it towards you, but there can be nothing away from the infinite and nothing can move towards it. Things move in relation to one another, but not in relation to the infinite. Thus when it is said that the infinite 'acts', no idea of motion on its part is implied.

We have every sympathy with the reader who may be wondering whether the foregoing description of the infinite is not after all a description of absolutely nothing, because the language throughout has been negative. The description amounts almost entirely to saying what the infinite is not. We have been 'outlining' it by the limits of space and time as one outlines the window with bricks.

'Clay is moulded into vessels,
And because of the space where nothing exists we
    are able to use them as vessels.
Doors and windows are cut out in the walls of a house,
And because they are empty space we are able to use them.'[3]

From the standpoint of reason and imagination this seeming nothingness of the infinite is inevitable. They can no more pic-

necessarily be. Therefore nowise can he be possibly. Therefore no potentiality is to be found in his essence.' St. Thomas, *Summa Contra Gentiles*, II.

[1] *Tao Te Ching*, xxxvii. Trs. Ch'u Ta-kao.
[2] *Isha Upanishad*. Trs. Juan Mascaro.
[3] *Tao Te Ching*, xi. Trs. Ch'u Ta-kao.

ture it than they can conceive the nature of the conscious Self by whose light and presence they are able to operate. Described in terms of reason and imagination, the conscious Self appears to be a mere void. Even the analogy of light fails, since light is an object of consciousness. It is like trying to describe a mirror in terms of the shapes and colours which it reflects. Yet as the mirror is the indispensable ground of the images, the conscious Self is the indispensable ground of knowledge, and the infinite of the finite universe. But as the mirror is known by touch (immediate contact) and the conscious Self by subjective intuition or immediate knowledge (and are thereby known as most real and effective), so metaphysical realization reveals the infinite as the absolutely effective and real cause, ground, and principle of life.

'Tao when uttered in words is so pure and void of flavour.
When one looks at it, one cannot see it;
When one listens to it, one cannot hear it.
However, when one uses it, it is inexhaustible.'[1]

A simple example of the effective power of the infinite when realized, is that one who knows the essential eternity of the Self has an enormously increased capacity for life, for the essence of metaphysical realization is the discovery that the conscious Self, the ultimate knower in man, is substantially identical with the infinite. Knowing his own essential eternity, man is able to *give* himself to life without stint or fear of loss, and this power is the secret of all creative work.

It will now be clear that the difference between the metaphysical and the religious viewpoints is that the former describes the infinite negatively in terms of what it is not, and the latter positively, in terms of what it is like. Described in terms of reason, feeling, and sense, the infinite is God. Because reason, feeling, and sense are human faculties, the God so described is necessarily anthropomorphic. This does not mean that religion has to think of God in the crudely anthropomorphic way, to picture Him as an old man with a white beard, but that it has to think of Him in terms of the human mind. The human senses picture Him in the form of the human Jesus—the physical embodiment of the divine mind.

There are the best precedents in the Catholic tradition for

[1] *Tao Te Ching*, xxxv. Trs. Ch'u Ta-kao.

# THE INFINITE AND THE FINITE

recognizing the distinction between the metaphysical and the strictly theological, or analogical, viewpoints. One of the most influential writers in the development of medieval theology was the sixth-century Syrian monk who wrote under the name of Dionysius the Areopagite. He distinguished between the *kataphatic* and the *apophatic* ways of knowing God, which are equivalent to the religious and the metaphysical. Kataphasis is the description of God in terms of created nature, and is the subject of St. Dionysius's treatise *The Divine Names*. Apophasis is the negative description, the subject of his *Mystical Theology*, whose final chapter might have been taken bodily from the Upanishads or Shankara.

'Going yet higher, we say that he (God) is neither a soul, nor a mind, nor an object of knowledge . . . neither is he reason, nor thought, nor is he utterable or knowable; neither is he number, order, greatness, littleness, equality, inequality, likeness, nor unlikeness; neither does he stand or move, nor is he quiescent; neither has he power, nor is power, nor light; neither does he live, nor is life; neither is he being, nor everlastingness, nor time . . . nor wisdom, nor one, nor oneness, nor divinity, nor goodness . . . nor any other thing known to us or to any other creature.'[1]

But the language of religion is kataphatic, for it confines itself to the temporal, spatial, and historical order. God is infinite in the sense of being at once indefinitely immense and indefinitely minute, for 'he whom the heaven of heavens cannot contain is found in the Virgin's womb'. He is eternal in the sense of everlasting; he lived *before* the creation of the universe and will continue to live forever *after* the end of the world, 'as it was in the beginning, is now, and ever shall be, through all the ages of ages'. Religion must also speak of the Beatific Vision and the life of heaven as coming after the end of the terrestrial order, as, in

---

[1] *Theologia Mystica*, V. The chapter is entitled, 'That he partakes not of intelligible things who is pre-eminently their maker'. Cf. *Mandukya Upanishad*, vii: The infinite consciousness 'is that which is not conscious of the subjective, nor that which is conscious of the objective, nor that which is conscious of both, nor that which is simple consciousness, nor that which is a mass all sentiency, nor that which is all darkness. It is unseen, transcendent, unapprehensible, uninferable, unthinkable, indescribable, the sole essence of the consciousness of Self, the negative of all illusion'. Trs. M. N. Dvivedi. In short, the ultimate Reality cannot be described in terms of any finite, or known, category.

the words of the Creed, 'the life of the world to come'. Likewise heaven is *above* the earth, beyond the firmament or *outside* space, even though 'outside' space the very word 'outside' is inapplicable.

Therefore theology enters into dangerous confusion when, as so frequently happens, it tries to mix religious and metaphysical concepts, attempting, for example, to relate a strictly eternal God to a religion so essentially historical as Christianity in a single frame of reference. For the historical side of Christianity to be kept in order, for the Incarnation, the Atonement, and the sacraments of the Church to retain their proper functions, one must be able to think of *celestial* as well as terrestrial history. The divine act of redemption, the Incarnation of God the Son, must be conceived as an event occurring in *time* not only from the terrestrial but also from the celestial viewpoints. If it occurs in time from the human standpoint alone, the Incarnation is no more than a revelation, an example of what God always is and does; it cannot be considered as an effective action of God which brings about an altogether new relationship between himself and the human race, unless God himself be held to be living in time. In the same way, if Baptism is to be regarded as an effective sign of the indwelling of God the Holy Spirit, the Spirit must be said to be doing something to the baptized person which He did not do before Baptism. For purposes of religion, the life of God must be considered in terms of time and space, albeit everlasting time and boundless space; eternity and infinity in the strict sense are outside the sphere of religious knowledge.

So long as Christianity was Hebraic in character there was no confusion of the religious and metaphysical orders. It is obvious that, with the exception of the Johannine literature, all Biblical writings conceive the life of God as indefinitely long and large. Actual eternity is a concept which enters definitively into Christian theology mainly through its contact with Neo-platonism. Theology has been muddled ever since, because, with the exception of popular Christianity, the metaphysical concept of eternity has been confused with the religious idea of perpetuity. Instead of realizing that the metaphysical viewpoint and language is different in principle from that of religion, the two were regarded as identical. The theologians therefore attempted to use both in one frame of reference, whereas if the frames of reference had been kept distinct, the true correspondence between them would have been apparent—the one in its entirety being seen to be an analogy of the other in its entirety.

This confusion, which has occurred in theologies other than the Christian, is responsible for one of the most misleading notions about metaphysical realization. It is apparent that powerful ideas, feelings, and sense-impressions are more or less mutually exclusive. In other words, it is practically impossible to concentrate on two ideas at once, or to experience two overwhelming emotions at once without hopeless psychic confusion. If, therefore, the intellectual knowledge of the infinite is confused with an idea, and more especially with a feeling, it will be presumed to *exclude* all other ideas and feelings. The person enjoying such knowledge will thus be expected to dismiss all finite impressions from his consciousness, and remain indefinitely suspended in a state of trance. It will be imagined that knowledge of the infinite is inconsistent with knowledge of the finite, and that he who would know the former must shun the latter, from which it is but a short step to thinking the infinite itself incompatible with finitude.

This misapprehension is strengthened by the negative language employed in metaphysical doctrine. Because the ultimate Reality is termed *in*finite, it is supposed to be a negation of the finite. It is difficult to escape the impression that in certain cases this misunderstanding is to be found in the Orient as well as in the Occident. Whenever this notion takes root, it becomes impossible to explain the existence of the finite at all, even as an illusion. If, as in debased forms of Hinduism as well as in certain kindred Western beliefs, the *maya* of the finite universe is regarded as having no origin in the infinite: if the world is pure illusion for which a purely illusory finite mind is alone responsible, we have an 'infinite regression' in which the finite is the illusion of an illusion. The teachings of the Vedanta about *maya* will always be liable to lead to this conclusion if it is not clearly understood that *maya* means illusion simply in the sense of something imagined *by the infinite*.[1]

[1] Cf. on the *Mandukya Upanishad* Gaudapada's *Karika*, 33. 'The absolute Advaita (non-dual Reality) imagines itself to be many; all objects are through it.' Shankara's gloss on this passage says, 'The ever real and one *atma* (Self) ... imagines itself as divided into many forms. And this notwithstanding its one and unique character. The meaning is this. No imagination can stand upon nothing; it must have a substratum to rest upon.'

Thus the infinite and the finite are incommensurable but perfectly compatible. The conscious Self, though not describable in terms of known objects, does not exclude objects. The mirror, without colour in itself, does not reject colour. Light, though essentially shapeless, does not obliterate shapes. On the contrary, the very fact that the Self, the mirror, and the light are objectless, colourless, and shapeless is what makes them able to entertain objects, colours, and shapes. This principle gives us the key to understanding the manifestation of the finite universe from the infinite.

The compatibility of the finite and the infinite has its religious counterpart in the Christian, and originally Hebraic, doctrine that the universe created by God is essentially good. The dualistic (and what was supposed to have been the Manichaean) doctrine that the finite universe is the work of an evil Demiurge and not of the good God presents no analogy with the metaphysical viewpoint. Nor has the 'mysticism' appropriate to the dualistic view any correspondence with metaphysical realization. Dualistic mysticism necessarily involves the absolute renunciation of natural acts and natural knowledge, and thus tends to an extreme asceticism. At the same time, metaphysic does not exclude asceticism or religious discipline, but would favour them (to the necessary degree) for the good of the body and mind rather than for the attainment or production of realization.

## [iii]

The problem of the manifestation of the finite from the infinite is a perennial philosophical puzzle. If the ultimate Reality is formless, how can it give birth to forms? If it is spaceless and timeless, how can it engender space and time? If it is imageless, how can it possibly imagine?

In actuality no contradiction exists here if it is remembered that the word *formless* as applied to the infinite does not signify the *opposite* of form. The true opposite of form is void—absolutely nothing. The word *formless* in this connection means 'transcending all possible forms'. For example, the colour red is in itself formless, but red may be used in drawing all possible forms. Red, though formless, is not the opposite of form. Similarly, the formal distinction of the spokes of a wheel is

*formless → transcending all forms.*

*ex nikilo nikil fit*

transcended at the hub; but there is no conflict between the formless unity of the hub and the formal diversity of spokes at the rim.

Thus when certain metaphysical doctrines describe the infinite as the No-thing, they most certainly do not mean that it is nothing. *Ex nihilo nihil fit*—something cannot come out of nothing. They mean simply that the infinite is not in the class of finite objects; that it is other than all known and knowable things. Nothing is the opposite and negation of something; but the infinite No-thing, so far from being the opposite of things, is their essential ground. The impossible problems raised by the Cartesian dualism of spirit and matter are the result of the dualism: spirit and matter must not be considered as opposites.

It is easy to think of the infinite as the ground of the finite in a purely passive sense. The problem is: how does the finite get into its ground? Where does the seed come from? Apparently the conscious Self does not produce the objects of its knowledge, but receives and reflects them passively from sense-impressions of an external world. Likewise the mirror does not itself engender its images; they are produced in it by things other than the mirror, and in the same way light does not create the shapes which it illumines, nor colour the forms it is used to paint. It seems that only forms and objects can give rise to forms and objects.

semantics

The problem, however, is created by the language and the analogies used. Language and thought, being finite faculties, are necessarily dualistic, and thus simply cannot escape setting up an opposition between the passive and the active, the ground and the objects, the knower and the known. It is then impossible to derive the one from the other, and the only way to get out of the dualism is to abolish one side of it—to say that only the ground is real, or that only the forms are real. This is the solution proposed by monism, whether spiritual (only the subjective is real) or material (only the objective is real).[1] But monism does not actually escape from dualism. Not only does it fail to

[1] To materialistic monism belong such current notions as behaviourism and mechanism, which attempt to reduce the experience of consciousness to the terms of the objects of which the observer is conscious. They have as much difficulty in explaining consciousness as an epiphenomenon of matter as the spiritualists in explaining matter as an epiphenomenon of consciousness.

answer the question: 'What is the origin of the *seeming* existence of the other side, if only one side is real?'—but also the very notion of absolute oneness is dualistic because it excludes and opposes the possibility of the many.

The difficulty is not solved by introducing some third term over and above the infinite and the finite, the knower and the known, the spiritual and the material. Because of the dualism inherent in thought, this would instantly suggest a fourth term, under and below the original pair of opposites, itself opposed to the third term.

In short, the difficulty is not to be solved in terms of language and rational thought at all, for in that these belong to the finite order they cannot possibly express the nature of the infinite. The solution lies only in the realm of metaphysical realization, not at all in the realm of theory.

The most that theory can say is this: the infinite and the finite, the knower and the known, are not to be considered as opposites, because opposition belongs only in the realm of the finite and the known. At the same time, the infinite is that which by definition *includes* the possibility of the finite, and the knower that which includes the possibility of the known. The infinite and the knower are not therefore passive as distinct from active. Activity and passivity are characteristics of finite and known objects. The knower does not actually reflect objects like a mirror, for a mirror, being an object, can be passive. Thus the infinite, considered as the knower or absolute Self of the finite universe, must be taken as omnipotent by definition, as necessarily including the possibility of knowing or imagining finite objects. If the infinite *could not* manifest the finite, it would be neither infinite nor omnipotent.

The word 'possibility' has been used advisedly, because the infinite does not *necessarily* include the finite. It is simply free to include it, or not to include it. The problem of how the infinite can engender the finite is, historically, an attempt to show that it *must* give birth to the finite, that there is a logical and necessary relationship between the two. The infinite is not the cause of the finite in the sense which the word 'cause' has come to acquire, in the sense that given a certain cause, a certain effect must of necessity follow. This is why it is easier to speak of the infinite as if it were a freely acting person, or God, than as if it were a simple force. In the following paragraphs we shall therefore have to use certain personal terms, such as willing and imagining, in discussing the creative activity of the infinite. But it must be remembered that such terms are analogy pure and simple. The limitations of thought are such that if we do not use these terms, the only other terms at our disposal are mechanistic, and would imply that the infinite causes the finite in the sense that the finite must *of necessity* be the result of the very being of the infinite. Alternatively, we should have to use language suggesting that the finite has no ground or origin in the infinite at all. For in trying to describe the ultimate Reality, man must either personalize it or degrade it to the sub-human. There is thus no harm in adopting the former way of description provided it be understood that the language is theological rather than metaphysical.

In strictly metaphysical language it is said that the infinite neither wills, imagines, acts, nor causes anything. But this gives the impression that it is merely inert and that the finite world simply causes itself, just as calling it the 'No-thing' gives the impression that it is nothing. Therefore negative language about the creative action of the infinite must be understood in the same way as negative language about its being and nature. It indicates, not privation, not nothingness and inertia, but an order of being and action superior to any human conception.

Self-abandonment, or, in religious language, selfless love, is the means whereby the infinite engenders the finite, though the act of self-abandonment implies no essential privation, and the act of engendering implies neither motion nor necessary causality. To put it in another way, the infinite 'produces' its object, the finite world, by giving itself to it, or imagining itself to be it. It does not distinguish or hold itself aloof from its object because there is no need whatever to do so. Being other than its object *in principle*, it can for that very reason afford to identify itself with the object. For example, if the eye were attempting to see itself, it would defeat itself; the eye sees by giving itself up to what it sees. The mind thinks, not by thinking itself, but by giving itself up to thoughts. The knower knows by identifying consciousness with its contents. It is for this reason that metaphysic so often appears to the uninformed as a kind of pantheism or monism, obliterating the principial distinction between the infinite and the finite. There is the fear that if the infinite is held to identify itself with the finite object it will in

66

some way lose its own infinity, and become immanent instead of transcendent. But the fear is groundless. Just because the infinite is *in essence* other than the finite, there is not the least need for it to insist on or cling to its own unique position. Without ceasing, then, to be infinite in the least degree, it manifests the finite universe by imagining itself to be every single finite object, by an abandoned and wholly unreserved absorption of itself in the life of everything that lives. Likewise, a mirror reflecting red at once becomes red and at the same time remains essentially silver, or colourless.

The frequent identification of the finite universe with the infinite *Brahma* which occurs in the Vedanta texts is not pantheism but the assertion that the infinite does not so transcend the finite as to exclude it. The difficulty of the Western mind in getting the finite 'out of' the infinite without resorting to pantheism is the result of putting the two in contrast or opposition. Only equals can be contrasted; only finite things can be opposed to one another. The problem is the result of the mind's inevitable tendency to conceive the infinite in finite terms, as 'embracing' the finite like space, as 'underlying' it like a passive ground, as 'preceding' it like something which is *first* a void, and *then* a void containing forms. The infinite is in no way separate from the finite, for the very idea of separation constitutes a limitation. The very contrast of the undetermined infinite on the one hand and the determined universe on the other puts the two on an equal basis which denies the transcendence of the infinite.

The moment we set the infinite in opposition to the finite, we destroy the finite: we get a conception of the infinite as a mere undifferentiated void from which the finite could never have arisen. To set the infinite apart from the finite, in the sense of opposition, is to deprive the universe of its being, to separate it from its ground. And very naturally it vanishes. To say that 'there is nothing infinite *apart* from finite things' is not to equate the universe with God, but simply to say that 'standoffishness', the finite quality of separation and opposition, is inapplicable to the infinite.

The same kind of difficulty has always bothered the theologian, for theology has never been able to give a satisfactory account of how God created the world, save that confession of ignorance—'out of nothing'. But the problem is manufactured by the way in which the question is asked. The theologian separates God from the world (as *prior* to it in time) and then wonders where the world came from and how. But in separating God from the world he not only destroys the world, but does something to God which cannot be done to him; he tries to push him away from an existing thing. To separate God from the world, the infinite from the finite, as *prior* to it in time, or as *outside* or *around* it in space, is only to bring God down into time, space, and finitude. And the moment you bring God into space and time, there is neither time nor space for anything else. God, the infinite, is only in space and time *as* everything else.

The ambiguity of language may give the impression that in saying that the infinite does not exist apart from the finite, we have been saying that its existence *depends* on that of the finite. On the contrary, the finite depends for its existence on the fact that the infinite is not apart from it, 'not-apartness' being a characteristic of the infinite alone.

The foregoing is not entirely expressible in religious terms because, as will be seen, the idea of God as the One keeps Him still within the sphere of dualism. He cannot therefore identify himself with his opposite, the Many. However, religion does insist on the absolute freedom of God, and thus regards the universe as his wholly gratuitous creation—not as the necessary effect of his being. Only in one unique respect does religion entertain the idea of God identifying himself with his creature by an act of *kenosis*, or self-abandonment, and that is in the Incarnation of the Christ, though there will be occasion to see that this very uniqueness has its metaphysical counterpart.

'Let this mind be in you, which you have in Christ Jesus, who, though he was in the form of God, did not count equality with God a thing to be grasped, but emptied himself, taking the form of a servant, being born in the likeness of men. And being found in human form he humbled himself and became obedient unto death.'[1]

The fact that this self-abandonment or self-emptying is designated of God the Son as distinct from the Father has a special significance from the metaphysical viewpoint, since the distinction between the Father and the Son corresponds to that between *Brahma* and *atma*, between the essentially unmanifested infinite and the infinite 'imagining itself' as the finite. Thus in

[1] Philippians, ii. 5-8.

theology God the Son, the Eternal Word or Wisdom, is the creative agent through whom all things are made. Principially distinct from the universe, he brings it into being because he identifies himself with it.

Religion must speak of the infinite as the One because reason cannot grasp the metaphysical doctrine of non-duality (*advaita*) as an idea; like infinity and eternity it is a negative expression or non-idea. Quite rightly, religion disavows any fellowship with pantheism or monism, any reduction of being to mere oneness. Its reason is that a doctrine of this type would destroy all finite values by denying to them any kind of reality. We have already shown that monism is just as repugnant to the metaphysical viewpoint, and for a similar reason—because it excludes and opposes the possibility of finite multiplicity. If, then, the infinite is not the opposite of the finite Many, it cannot be called the One as opposed to the Many. One and Many are both terms of number, and thus of finitude and dualism. Hence the infinite must be called the non-dual rather than the One.

'God is an essence without duality (*advaita*), or as some maintain, without duality but not without relations (*visishthadvaita*). He is only to be apprehended as Essence (*asti*), but his Essence subsists in a two-fold nature (*dvaitibhava*); as being and as becoming.'[1]

Because One and Many are opposed, if the Many are reduced to the One they disappear; if the One is reduced to the Many it disappears. But one and many can be reduced to the non-dual because, while they exclude each other, the non-dual includes them both. Just because the non-dual is not opposed to the finite manifold universe, it can become it without losing or ceasing to be itself. Because the non-dual infinite includes the possibility of the finite, of the object, of the other, it includes the possibility of significant relationships, of value, of personality, of lover and beloved. But the merely One would exclude such possibilities, and for this reason religion, if pushed too far, is in much greater danger of monism than metaphysic. For as soon as religion begins to think about the one God existing prior to the universe, it begins to slip into monism. Here is the one God all by himself, with no reality other than his own essence. Is not this the purest monism? If God becomes Love and Con-

[1] A. K. Coomaraswamy, *Hinduism and Buddhism* (New York, 1943), p. 10.

sciousness only by finding the necessary object for loving and knowing in his created universe, we are making the universe necessary to God, and is not this the purest pantheism?

The idea of the Trinity saves Christianity from the monistic predicament. It gives God significance even prior to the universe, because he always contains both the subject and the object of his own love, the everlasting I-Thou relationship of the Father and the Son in the bond of the Holy Spirit of love. Thus the Trinity comes as close as the language of religion permits to the doctrine of non-duality, for the One is seen as including Three, the Unity as not opposed to diversity.

It is generally supposed in the West that the Vedanta doctrine of non-duality, being a monism, entirely excludes the values of worship, of the I-Thou relation between man and God, and makes the supreme spiritual ideal the total absorption and disappearance of the human person into an undifferentiated oneness. This impression is the result of trying to understand the Vedanta from the religious viewpoint. The doctrine of non-duality is as consistent with worship, as an expression of love and relationship, as it is with the existence of the entire finite and dual order. Because human reason, feeling, and sense can never grasp the truth of non-duality, they must relate themselves to the infinite analogically. Metaphysical realization, which occurs in the intellect, neither displaces reason, feeling, and sense, nor attempts to raise them to its own level. As an intellectual being, man can realize himself as the *atma*, the infinite imagining itself finite. But as a being of reason, feeling, and sense, man must relate himself to the infinite as to a God *other* than himself.[1] A supposed *feeling* of identity with the infinite is nothing more than a dangerous psychic inflation; not being able to grasp the infinite, the finite faculty of feeling will 'burst' if it attempts to do so.[2]

[1] Thus not all Shankara's alleged monism prevented him from writing a considerable number of hymns in the *bhakti* or devotional style which, with a mere alteration of names, would perfectly express the worship of a Christian, Jewish, or Islamic theist.

[2] Many Western persons are so identified with their own feelings, and so unobjective about them, that they will find this point of view strange. They cannot imagine anything but the feeling faculty as their deepest centre, and therefore cannot accept its strictly peripheral and objective status. Thus they would judge a worship looked at from the metaphysical viewpoint as insincere, since they cannot

# THE INFINITE AND THE FINITE

The notion of absorption, of an ultimate and ideal obliteration of the finite in the infinite, is equally foreign to oriental metaphysic, and is the result of our imposing the religious idea of everlastingness on the metaphysical concept of eternity. A realization of eternity does not involve any leaving of the finite behind, because from the eternal standpoint all time is present. There can thus be no idea of passing out of the finite into the infinite in the order of temporal succession. A *nirvana* in which finite existence belonged solely to the *past* would not be a true realization at all, but, on the contrary, a strictly temporal state.

'Those who, afraid of the sufferings arising from the discrimination of birth-and-death (*samsara*), seek for Nirvana, do not know that birth-and-death and Nirvana are not to be separated from one another; and, seeing that all things subject to discrimination have no (absolute) reality, (they) imagine that Nirvana consists in the future annihilation of the senses and their fields.'[1]

Buddhism expresses this truth in the Bodhisattva doctrine, which is that the highest spiritual degree is not that of the *pratyeka-buddha*, the person who escapes from the cycle of transmigration into *nirvana*, but of the Bodhisattva who, realizing the essential unity of the cycle and *nirvana*, continues to live indefinitely in the cycle for the enlightenment of all other beings. This is, indeed, an exoteric doctrine, expressing the profounder metaphysical principle that the finite and the infinite are not incompatible, and that eternity does not involve the cessation or obliteration of events in time. The Western religious equivalent is the doctrine of the resurrection of the body.

'To darkness are they doomed who worship only the body, and to greater darkness they who worship only the spirit.

'Worship of the body (the finite) alone leads to one result, worship of the spirit (the infinite) leads to another. So we have heard from the wise.

'They who worship both the body and the spirit, by the body overcome death, and by the spirit achieve immortality.'[2]

believe that a man is really feeling when he is objective about his feelings. For the same reason, persons of this nature are an easy prey to psychic inflation when they become involved with mysticism or oriental metaphysic.

[1] *Lankavatara Sutra*, 2, xviii. Trs. Suzuki. (London, 1932), p. 55. Cf. *Atharvaveda*, 10, vii, which speaks of the state 'wherein what hath been and shall be, and all worlds are instant (*prati-tisthata*)'.

[2] *Isha Upanishad*. Trs. Prabhavananda and Manchester.

# THE INFINITE AND THE FINITE

The true end of man according to metaphysical doctrine is the realization of the Supreme Identity of *atma* and *Brahma*, of the Self and the infinite. This is to be described in detail in the next chapter, but it must be introduced here because of its importance for the understanding of non-duality. Man as the object of his own knowledge is the ego or soul (*jiva*); as the subject, the knower, or the Self (*atma*) he is in reality one with the infinite or *Brahma*. Man as the Self is the infinite in the act of identifying itself with the finite ego.

But the realization of the Supreme Identity, of the truth that the Self is the infinite and not the ego, does not involve the obliteration of the ego and of finite experience. Passages in the Vedanta texts which might give this impression by saying that, from the standpoint of the Supreme Identity, the world is seen as nothing, as illusion, and that objects are no more, must not be understood from the temporal point of view. They do not mean that the eternal state of realization is a disappearance or absorption of the finite *subsequent* to its appearance and manifestation.

The point is simply that while the finite remains real, in the light of supreme knowledge, of the *infinite* Reality, the finite is *by comparison* nothing. As a relative reality it remains, but it has no more power to limit or conceal the infinite than nothing at all. Its effect upon the infinite is as if it were not. The image of sugar in a mirror is actually there, but so far as sweetening the mirror is concerned its effect is nil, as if it were not there. Almost the same idea is expressed by St. Augustine:

'I beheld these others beneath Thee, and saw that they neither altogether are, nor altogether are not. An existence they have, because they are from Thee; and yet no existence, because they are not what Thou art. For only that really is that remains unchangeably. . . . Thou, Lord, madest them, who art beautiful, for they are beautiful; who art good, for they are good; who art, for they are. Yet are they not beautiful, nor good, nor are they, as Thou their Creator art—compared with whom, they are neither beautiful, nor good, nor are.'[1]

Likewise oriental metaphysic does not, as is so often alleged, entail a 'denial of the value of personality' save on the principle that 'he that humbleth himself shall be exalted' and 'he that loseth his soul shall find it'. In common with Christian tradi-

[1] *Confessions*, 7, xi and 11, iv.

tion, it recognizes that the more personality is subordinated to the infinite and 'denied', the more intensely personal and unique it becomes. It is only in quite recent times that Christians have 'valued personality' in the sense of trying to develop it self-consciously, both in themselves and in their ideas of God, a procedure as ineffectual as trying to make pictures do duty for windows. Only when the mind and soul is empty, like clear glass, does it let through the light of God. It is surely the veriest truism that those who aim at greatness do not achieve greatness, and that those who strive for happiness do not find happiness. Personality flowers according to the same principle.

The doctrine of the Supreme Identity does not and should not come within the sphere of religion, for it has already been shown that it cannot be realized from the standpoint of reason, feeling, or sensation. Translated improperly into their terms it becomes pantheism or monism, whereas the proper translation is religious theism. The difficulty which the religious mind so often experiences in accepting the metaphysical standpoint is that either reason, feeling, or, sometimes, sensation is very frequently identified so closely with the Self that it is held to be the deepest level of man's being. In the Western world it so happens that feeling is more usually identified with the Self than any other faculty, for which cause the feeling element in religion—moral value, ecstasy, consolation—is apt to be regarded, not as analogy of the ultimate Reality, but as its very essence. This predominance of what Guénon terms the 'sentimental' element in religion gives the modern Christian a standpoint from which metaphysic seems cold, amoral, and impersonal, if not absolutely meaningless.

In conclusion, therefore, it must be repeated that intellectual knowledge of the non-dual and of the Supreme Identity does not deny the value and reality of the finite realm in any of its aspects. Words such as 'cold' and 'impersonal' denote qualities having opposites, and are thus inapplicable to the infinite. On the contrary, the infinite is not only not opposed to the finite, but, as the very principle and origin of its being, orders the natural universe to its own proper perfection, which is to represent the infinite by analogy. *Unum quodque tendens in suam perfectionem tendit in divinam similitudinem.*[1]

---

[1] St. Thomas, *Contra Gentiles*, III, xxi. 'Whatever tends to its own perfection tends to a divine likeness.'

# II. THE SUPREME IDENTITY

## OUTLINE

1. The mystery of man's true identity, of who or what is the ultimate *knower* in man, is a problem inaccessible to both science and religion.

Theology confuses this identity (the spirit or Self) with the soul or ego (the known individual), because theology deals in objective concepts, and the Self cannot become the *object* of its own knowledge. Metaphysic realizes the Supreme Identity of the Self and the infinite Reality.

2. The Self is the supra-individual ground of man's consciousness, the indeterminate field or continuum in which all his experiences exist. It abandons itself freely to these experiences, because the Self is the infinite in the act of manifesting or identifying itself with the finite. The distinction from solipsism and the psychological unconscious. Manifestation as the 'play' of the infinite.

3. Religious objections to this doctrine as annihilating any significant relationship between man and God, cannot be sustained without destroying the meaningful relation between the Father and the Son in the doctrine of the Trinity. If the Supreme Identity destroys the meaning of reality, so does *any* idea of God.

## II. THE SUPREME IDENTITY

Of all the mysteries of the external world, of wonders seen with the eyes, heard with the ears, or touched with the hands, nothing is so profound an enigma as the internal mystery of man's own identity. Certain as we may be of the reality of our own being, its nature and origin elude us to exasperation. Here is one problem to which physiology, biology, and psychology offer no clue at all, for explore as they may into the objects of human knowledge, the knowing subject behind the eye behind the microscope is more remote from observation than the other side of the moon. In reading even theology one cannot escape the impression that more, far more, is known and taught of the nature of God himself than of the impenetrable being within who can say, 'I am'.

At some time every one of us has paused with something like awe to contemplate the weird riddle of who we would have been if our fathers had married someone else. Or we have tried to imagine without the slightest avail the prospect of total annihilation after death. Or we have wondered why I am myself and not John or Mary, and what it would be like to see the world through someone else's eyes. Perhaps the most fascinating of these questions is the thought of death as possible annihilation, as the absolute disappearance of that central point of being upon which all our knowledge of existence depends.

If death is the complete obliteration of awareness, we shall become as if we had never been. Experience, and memory with it, will vanish into a total blank; past, present, and future will, from the only standpoint of knowledge we have ever had, be entirely non-existent. We shall return into the void which preceded our birth, and the episode between will be as much a nothing as death itself. Granted that consciousness cannot imagine its own dissolution, problems enough remain.

If we were once absolutely not before birth, and we become again absolutely not after death, is there not then the chance

76

that our identity may emerge from the darkness yet again, employing, perhaps, some other body and mind, with no memory even of former existence? We are sure enough that after we die other identities will look out upon the world, and that for them time, space, and history will continue. What, then, is the difference between those identities and ours? Every one of them senses itself as the central point of the universe and the sole vessel of knowledge. Every one of them has an inescapable intuition of the Self as a mystery deeper than and distinct from the external individuality of body, senses, feelings, and thoughts, as something which could equally well inhabit *another* individual system, with other memories, other characteristics, other experiences. Is there, indeed, any real difference between saying, on the one hand, that after death I am born again with no memory of the past, or, on the other hand, that after my death another person is born? Is there any real difference between my conscious Self and anyone else's, or is the difference simply that there is but one conscious Self taking innumerable different points of view?

It is easy enough to say that the sense of identity, of being conscious, is merely the integrated sensitivity of a particular physical organism, and that since each organism is unique, once dissolved that particular integration of sensitivity is as absolutely finished and past as the physical organism itself. But to reduce the Self to a mere phenomenon of organic chemistry is to reduce the reduction likewise. If the sense of a selfhood *independent* of the body is a mere chemical illusion, what makes the very opinion that this is so any less of an illusion? Common as such opinions may be among persons with some scientific training, they are conjecture pure and simple. Reasonably sure as we may be that surgical operations on the brain can change character, and that physiological disturbances can wipe out whole areas of memory, there remains the intuition of the Self as the simple Witness of character and memory as *objective* experiences in the psycho-physical organism.

It is possible, likewise, to say that all these questions have no meaning since the conscious Self is no more than the aggregate of countless specific impressions. Consciousness is nothing other than this sensation called blue sky, that nervous disturbance called fear, this impression called square box, and that experience called toothache. Consciousness is never found apart from some such specific impression; hence it *is* these impressions. Yet no one has ever seen a mirror that was not reflecting some particular set of images, and nevertheless there is a distinction between mirror and images. Furthermore it is a verbal confusion to suggest that impressions, sensations, and experiences are themselves conscious. A camera receives impressions, and is not unlike the human eye. A calculating machine resembles still more the complex gadget behind the eye, the human brain, and can solve problems which many brains cannot master. It is not beyond the bounds of physical possibility that we might construct some vast thinking-machine which could reproduce every cerebral operation. But can such contraptions ever *know* that they are thinking and being impressed?

From the scientific standpoint there can be no answer at all, for it is idle to suppose that the thinking process can transcend itself—much less explain something which in turn transcends thinking, that *awareness* of the mechanical process of the brain which the calculating machine does not enjoy. This is the reason for the failure of all merely speculative, theoretic, and rational 'metaphysics'. There can be no rational reconstruction of that which transcends and illumines reason—consciousness. The rational process is mechanical, and, like every machine, if an attempt is made to make it transcend itself, it only goes round in circles. The conscious Self transcends thought, but it cannot fully reconstruct itself, or its knowledge of thought, in terms of thought, just as an artist cannot reconstruct himself or his full understanding of art upon canvas.

Because, then, the conscious Self is beyond the reach of rational analysis, it is really absurd not to accept its basic 'intuitions' without quibble as if they were the most certain kind of knowledge that we have. There is first the intuition of its own timelessness or eternity, and, second, not perhaps quite so strong in all people, of its transcendence of the individual order, of its potential interchangeability with any other conscious Self. For if at least the first of these intuitions is not true, we shall never know that it is not! If it is to be verified at all, the verification must be positive.

Now this universal and inescapable intuition of persons who practise any sort of introspection, this intuition of the interior conscious Self, distinct from every known object including thoughts and feelings, space and time, is, as it were, the germ of metaphysical realization. The connection is suggested in a familiar passage from Tennyson's *Memoirs*:

'. . . A kind of waking trance I have frequently had, quite up from my boyhood, when I have been all alone. This has generally come upon me through repeating my own name two or three times to myself silently, till all at once, as it were out of the intensity of the consciousness of individuality, the individuality itself seemed to dissolve and fade away into boundless being; and this is not a confused state, but the clearest of the clearest, the surest of the surest, the weirdest of the weirdest, utterly beyond words, where death was an almost laughable impossibility, the loss of personality (if so it were) seeming no extinction, but the only true life.'[1]

When we go to religion for light on the nature of the conscious Self it is found that Catholic doctrine, for instance, virtually avoids the question. Man is viewed as a dichotomy of body and soul, the latter being defined as an intellectual substance entirely uncompounded and simple in nature, and lacking all corporeal qualities such as size, colour, and shape. In practice, the soul is identified with the Self, as with the spirit of the Pauline trichotomy—body, soul, and spirit. One wonders what has happened to spirit in the development of Catholic theology. It seems either to have been confused with the soul, or to have been left out of consideration altogether so that man may be defined in terms of every aspect of his nature *except* the spirit, with the implication, perhaps, that spirit is more than man. According to the Council of Constantinople (A.D. 869):

'Both the Old and the New Testament teach that man has one rational and intellectual soul (μίαν ψυχὴν λογικήν τε καὶ νοερὰν). . . . Some have been impious enough to assert, quite impudently, that man has two *souls*. This sacred and ecumenical council . . . vehemently anathematizes the inventors of such impiety. . . . If anyone shall presume to act contrary to this definition, let him be anathema.'[2]

This is understood by later theologians to mean that man consists of but two essential elements, the rational soul (*anima rationalis*) and the body (*corpus humanum*). But the conciliar definition says only that man does not have two *souls*; it says

---

[1] *Memoirs of Alfred, Lord Tennyson*, vol. ii, p. 473.
[2] Denzinger, *Enchiridion*, p. 338.

nothing about spirit as a third factor entirely different in principle from a soul, a distinction upon which several passages in the New Testament insist quite plainly. Thus in Hebrews iv. 12 we have, 'For the word of God is living and active, sharper than any two-edged sword, piercing to the division of soul and spirit'. Or again in 1 Corinthians xv. 44-45, 'It is sown a psychic body; it is raised a spiritual body. If there is a psychic body, there is also a spiritual body. Thus it is written, The first man Adam became a living soul. The last Adam became a life-giving spirit.' Even more to the point is 1 Corinthians ii. 14-15, 'The psychic man (i.e. the soul) does not receive the things of the Spirit of God, for (as things metaphysical) they are folly to him, and he is not able to understand them (except by analogy) because they are spiritually discerned. The spiritual man (i.e. the Self) discerns all things, but himself is not to be discerned by anyone. For, Who has known the mind of the Lord, so as to instruct him?'[1] There is the suggestion, too, that St. Paul associates the spirit with the conscious Self, 'for who knoweth the things of the man except the spirit of the man which is in him?'[2]

In view of these rather clear distinctions between spirit and soul, it seems strange that later theology has either confused the two or merely left the spirit out of consideration. St. Thomas's description of the soul seems to involve such a confusion with the spirit. On the one hand he identifies the soul with the intellect, the knower or principle of knowledge.

'It must necessarily be allowed that the principle of intellectual operation, which we call the soul of man, is a principle both incorporeal and subsistent. For it is clear that by means of the intellect man can know all corporeal things. Now whatever knows certain things *cannot have any of them in its own nature,*

---

[1] The contrast of the psychic and the spiritual man (πνευματικὸς ἄνθρωπος) might be taken superficially to refer to two different kinds of persons, but St. Paul uses the same type of expression (Ephesians iv.24: τὸν καινὸν ἄνθρωπον) of a state or level of man's interior life. Most translations distort the force of the contrast between soul and spirit by rendering psychic (ψυχικὸς) as 'natural' or even 'physical'. Cf. also Ecclesiastes xii. 7: 'Then the dust shall return to the dust as it was: and the spirit (ruach) to God who gave it'. In Hebrew ruach differs from nefesh, the soul, or 'the man himself', in having a divine and supra-individual character.

[2] 1 Corinthians ii. 11.

because that which is in it naturally would impede the knowledge of anything else.'[1]

Thus far his description of the *soul* is actually a description of *spirit*, of a transcendent and metaphysical entity distinct from the objects of knowledge. But at the same time he wants to make the intellect a power of the soul, of a soul having affections, qualities, and individual character. If, however, the soul has a distinct character and knows its own character, how can it be said that 'whatever knows certain things cannot have any of them in its own nature'?

On the other hand, therefore, St. Thomas is forced to associate what the soul knows of itself with the body. The intellect does not know itself or the motions of the soul directly; it knows them in terms of sensible images or *phantasms*—'the images of particular things, impressed on or preserved by the bodily organs'. Thus the *known* soul becomes an aspect of the body, the soul in itself remaining one with the intellect. The immediate objects of intellectual knowledge are physical, and indeed the intellect has nothing physical in its nature; but because the phantasms reflect the acts and qualities of the intellectual soul, the intellect has an indirect knowledge of itself in physical terms. However, the metaphysical principle that 'whatever knows certain things cannot have *any* of them in its own nature' should strictly refer to the qualities reflected as well as to the sensible images or phantasms which bear them.

It would be simpler, then, to give man a threefold structure: the body as the physical aspect or expression of the soul; the soul as man's known or knowable psychic life—affections, ideas, feelings, and sensations; and the intellect as the knowing subject or spirit. For a theologian this would seem a perfectly scriptural classification, silent as scripture may be on the exact nature of spirit. But St. Thomas insists that the intellect (spirit) must be in and of the soul. 'The separate intellect, according to the teaching of our Faith, is God himself, who is the soul's Creator, and only beatitude',[2] and therefore if the intellect or

---

[1] *Summa Theologica*, I. Q. 75, art. 2. The sense of the last sentence is apparently that if, say, the eyes were always to look through red glass or were themselves dyed red, they would be unable to recognize the distinction of red from other colours.

[2] *Summa Theol.*, I. Q. 79, art. 4.

consciousness in man is distinct from the soul it must be God's *own* consciousness.[1]

It is probably true that the great majority of people naturally identify soul with spirit, their thoughts and feelings with the conscious Self which knows them. In common speech we say, 'I *am* afraid', whereas a more introspective language would say, 'I am aware of a fear'. Because of this general and habitual confusion of psychic experience with the conscious Self, any suggestion that the Self is divine would give the impression of saying that the individual soul is God, which is obviously absurd. Thus the identification of spirit with soul in theology reflects the common state of the human mind, and the very function of religion is to speak in terms adapted to this state. When spirit and soul are identified, God must be extraverted, must be understood as One 'outside' and 'beyond' lest he likewise be identified with the individual soul.

It is for this reason, then, that, apart from the opinions of individual theologians, religion gives no dogmatic definition of the nature of the conscious Self or of the spirit in man. It defines man as soul and body; it does not define him in so far as he is one who *knows* soul and body, since man at the level of the interior knower-of-himself is indefinable; at this point he belongs to the metaphysical order, which is beyond the strictly religious sphere. The conscious Self cannot be formulated in terms of the soul, in terms of ideas, feelings and sensations, because it transcends them. In so far, then, as religion is dogma, a body of formal and positive propositions, it must speak entirely in 'soul-language', and thus cannot speak of the Self without, on the one hand, identifying it with the soul, and, on the other, projecting it externally as the positively defined God.

If we look without avail to science, philosophy, and religion for light on the mysterious nature of the Self, it is otherwise with traditions of the metaphysical order. Their answer is not without its problems, but with complete assurance and unanimity it is that the Self in man and the infinite Self are identical.

[1] That this is St. Thomas's meaning is clear also from *Objection 1* in the same article: 'It would seem that the agent intellect is not something in the soul. For the effect of the agent intellect is to give light for the purpose of understanding. But this is done by something higher than the soul, according to John, i. 9: *He was the true light that enlighteneth every man coming into this world.* Therefore the agent intellect is not something in the soul.'

'An invisible and subtle essence is the Spirit of the whole universe. That is Reality. That is Truth. Thou art That (*tat tvam asi*).'[1]

'The *atma*, the Self, is never born and never dies. It is without a cause and is eternally changeless. It is beyond time, unborn, permanent, and eternal. It does not die when the body dies. Concealed in the heart of all beings lies the *atma*, the Spirit, the Self; smaller than the smallest atom, greater than the greatest spaces.'[2]

'Therefore "*There is no deity but ALLAH*" is the Many's declaration of Unity: that of the Few is "*There is no he but HE*"; the former is more general, but the latter is more particular, more comprehensive, more exact, and more apt to give to him who declares it entrance into the pure and absolute Oneness and Onliness.'[3]

'To gauge the soul we must gauge it with God, for the Ground of God and the Ground of the Soul are one and the same. . . . There is a spirit in the soul, untouched by time and flesh, flowing from the Spirit, remaining in the Spirit, itself wholly spiritual. In this principle is God, ever verdant, ever flowering in all the joy and glory of his actual Self. . . . It is free of all names and void of all forms. It is one and simple, as God is one and simple, and no man can in any wise behold it.'[4]

Quotations of this kind might be multiplied indefinitely, from India, from China, from the Sufis of Islam, and from the contemplatives of Europe. Familiar as this theme has become to students of 'comparative religions', it is unhappily true that the great majority of its modern interpreters and commentators fail to get the meaning of it, and thus present it in a way that is absolutely repugnant to the religious tradition of the West.

'Within a cultural milieu (*Kulturkreis*) where certain conceptions (which once had or still have a wider meaning amongst other peoples) have been limited and specialized, it is daring to give to this conclusion the simple wording that it requires.

[1] *Chandogya Upanishad*, vi. 13. Trs. Juan Mascaro.
[2] *Katha Upanishad*.
[3] Al-Ghazzali, *Mishkat Al-Anwar*. Trs. W. H. T. Gairdner (London, 1924), p. 64.
[4] Meister Eckhart. Note that the *ground* of the soul, i.e., the Self or spirit, is one and the same, not with God, but with the *ground* of God, i.e., with the metaphysical as distinct from the analogical and externalized ultimate Reality.

## THE SUPREME IDENTITY

In Christian terminology to say: "Hence I am God Almighty" sounds both blasphemous and lunatic.'[1]

It must be understood, then, that the Self, the *atma* which is *Brahma*, is not to be confused with the empirical ego, with the soul-body wherewith the conscious Self is normally identified. Furthermore the infinite Reality which constitutes the Self is not, save by analogy, the external, positively described space-time God of religion. The principle *tat tvam asi* does *not* imply the consequence, 'Hence I, John Smith, am God Almighty'! For John Smith is the known and designated individual, distinguishable from others, which the conscious Knower actually transcends. Between metaphysic and religion there is no possible point of conflict, since religious language can only define man as he is known, not as he is knower.

### [ii]

By simple introspection we may come to a preliminary understanding of what is meant by the Self as distinct from the ego or particular individuality. This understanding will, however, be in the nature of a 'non-idea', because we shall have to think of the Self in terms of what it is not. We begin with the principle that there is a distinction (not of opposition, but of transcendence) between subject and object, knower and known. A light illumines things other than itself, and the eye sees things other than itself; what is seen, then, is not the seer.

Man is aware of his own body, potentially if not actually. By sight and touch he can know its whole exterior surface, and by internal sensations, by pains in the head and other organs, by moods and emotions, by dreams and other psycho-physical phenomena, he becomes aware of its interior functioning. An emotion, for example, is a true 'feeling' of the inside of the brain; one does not have to get at it with the fingers! If he has physiological knowledge he can concentrate attention or interior feeling on almost any organ in the physical system.[2] In the same

[1] Erwin Schrödinger, *What is Life?* (New York, 1946), p. 88.
[2] Such awareness is cultivated to an extreme degree in the practice of *hatha-yoga*, which involves a somewhat sensational degree of control over the muscular, respiratory, nervous, and circulatory systems. The object of *hatha-yoga*, aside from mere physical culture, is to acquire a very thorough knowledge of the distinction of the Self from the internal organs.

way he is, or can be, aware of the psychological patterns of thought and feeling which constitute his individual character—his ideas, emotions, and desires—constituting the soul. In sensing, feeling, thinking, he knows, not 'I am sensing, feeling, thinking,' but 'I am aware of the senses, the feelings, and the mind interacting with their objects'.

Now what John Smith himself, or any other person, recognizes as John Smith is not that which knows. It is precisely this complex of known or knowable objects, or some aspect thereof. But the knowing subject, as distinct from the known objects, does not have the characteristics of John Smith. Indeed, it does not have any physical, emotional, or ideational characteristics at all; it is knowing pure and simple, and this is that mysterious identity which can neither be made an object of knowledge nor imagined as permanently annihilated.

Although some of us are accustomed to thinking of the knowing subject as a *centre*, as a sort of spark from which light irradiates, it would seem more correct to think of it as a *field*. Known objects are in one sense distinct from it, but at the same time they are *in* it. That is to say, everything that we know is known *in* our consciousness. As is well recognized, we have no knowledge of an external world, of distances between our bodies and other things, or of moving from one place to another, as anywhere but *within* the field of our own awareness. In other words, while we speak of knowing the external world only through impressions made on our minds and senses from outside, the very concept or sense of externality and the very existence of the sense-organs are themselves known only within consciousness. This fact, once it is noticed by introspection, is utterly unavoidable even though unfamiliar and disconcerting. We are merely unaccustomed to it through thinking of consciousness as a centre located in the body, rather than a field with a central node.

The fact that all things are within consciousness implies neither solipsism nor the unreality of objects. So far as the relative reality of individuals and objects is concerned, it matters not whether we call them events within a space-time continuum, or events within a field of consciousness. It is not difficult to conceive consciousness as a field in which there may be an indefinite number of nodes or points of view, each of which corresponds to the vaguely restricted area which every one of us calls 'my' consciousness. Space and time will themselves be functions of the field, and every point of view or node within the field will, like stars in space, be central relative to the others.

> ' "Where," said the king, "O where? I have not found it!"
> "Here," said the dwarf, and music echoed "Here"!
> This infinite circle hath no line to bound it,
> Therefore its deep strange centre is everywhere!'[1]

Those who take the naïve standpoint that consciousness is a function of 'physical matter' (and what on earth *is* 'physical matter', and where is it save in consciousness?) are impressed by the observation that 'inorganic' structures predate living organisms by incalculable periods of time, and that consciousness is therefore a sort of incidental top layer of fungus upon the age-old rock of matter. But we must take account of the fact that distance in time is as much a phenomenon within consciousness as distance in space. Furthermore, if the word 'evolution' means anything at all, it denotes not the building of a tower to which more or less unessential trimmings are added when the main edifice is complete, but the unfolding, the outward volution of properties contained within the structure from the beginning. What, therefore, appears latest in time upon the surface will, so far from being unessential and superficial, be properties of the most deeply ingrained and fundamental order. Evolution is 'matter' turning itself inside out so as to manifest its deepest powers, the things most interior and essential to its nature.

Transposing, then, our concept of consciousness as an infinite field containing innumerable nodes from electro-magnetic into metaphysical language, we see that the field is *Brahma*, the infinite Reality, and the field *in the act* of containing nodes, or points of view, is the Self or *atma*. Each node, or point of view, taken by the non-dual and undivided Self is the intellect or *buddhi*. To change our metaphor, the *buddhi* resembles a ray from the central sun of the Self. Within each ray or point of view, the Self projects the various objects of finite experience, and, in doing so, identifies itself with them—or at least with

[1] Alfred Noyes, *The Unknown God* (New York, 1940), p. 252. The stanza is based on the traditional conception of the infinite as 'that circle whose centre is everywhere and whose circumference is nowhere'.

those more proximate objects, the contents of the soul, which constitute the ego or *jivatma*.

The process may be clarified by retracing it backwards. The ego (*jivatma*) consists of man's 'inner' life in so far as it can be made an *object* of knowledge; it is the complex of sensation, reason, feeling, character, and memory—in short, the soul. The consciousness which *knows* this object is principially the Self. But in so far as this consciousness is limited in range, in so far as it is a point of view having a restricted area of experience, it is the *buddhi*, the ray or viewpoint taken by the Self. Thus the Self manifests the individual by identifying itself with a point of view and with objects in that point of view, with the *buddhi* and the *jivatma*. However, while identifying itself with these, it remains in principle infinite and identical with *Brahma*. As such it retains a total 'viewpoint' or omniscience which, of course, does not penetrate through to the various 'rays' and, much less, to the egos which they contain.[1]

Stripped of technicalities, all that we are saying is that the basic awareness in man, the fundamental identity and knower, is a point of view taken by that essentially infinite and omniscient consciousness which is the ultimate Reality. Consciousness in man is continuous with, and in principle identical with, the All-consciousness. So far from being a mere superstructure of the material universe, consciousness is its very ground. In our own central identity we know Reality intimately and immediately; elsewhere we see only its outer shell.

As theory alone, something not unlike this has been found in Western philosophy, divorced however from any proper concept of non-duality. It must be repeated, therefore, that the metaphysical doctrine as found in the Vedanta and elsewhere does not rest on theory but on realization. The proposition *tat tvam asi*, the Self is the infinite, is based on an experience of its

[1] The foregoing explanation of the manifestation of the ego from the Self employs a simplified version of the terminology of the Vedanta. In Mahayana Buddhism the same principles are expressed with certain differences in terminology and classification. *Brahma* and *atma* are termed respectively *Amala-vijnana* and *Alaya-vijnana*. In the Mahayana sutras the term *atma* almost invariably denotes the ego, the complex of *samskara* (dreams and creative ideas), *samjna* (percepts and concepts), and *vedana* (discriminatory feeling). The term *buddhi* is sometimes employed in the same sense as in the Vedanta.

truth. When the Self is no longer identified with the ego, when, in certain spiritual practices, it penetrates and realizes its own depths, it simply *knows* that it is eternal and all-inclusive. Words can convey no proof, no conviction, of this experience. But, when realized, this knowledge is of a certainty so much greater than any other kind of knowledge that doubt seems impossible.

Because there is not the slightest possibility that an experience of this kind can be checked by scientific instruments, it can be criticized only from the standpoint of theory.[1] One can only say that it seems unreasonable, or that one does not like the idea. We shall therefore have to content ourselves with showing that it is not unreasonable, but that, on the contrary, it continues to give light beyond that point where other doctrines lapse into contradictions compared with which even paradox is clarity. Beyond that remains the supremely important matter of describing the preparations for realization, wherein lies the only satisfactory means of verification.

It is true, of course, that lunatics claim to experience things which, to them, are so certain that doubt is unthinkable. Thus it is often suggested that realization of the Supreme Identity is simply another form of delusion or psychic obsession resulting from excessive introspection. To this it is only necessary to give the old answer, that whereas the delusions of insanity make their victims impossible to live with, we shall discover that knowledge of the Supreme Identity, of man's relation to his true end, is something which we cannot live without. If this kind of thing is insanity, then, as Jung has well said, life itself 'is a disease with a very bad prognosis; it lingers on for years to end with death'.

If, then, man's basic consciousness is a viewpoint of the eternal Self, the question arises as to what becomes of the Self in the state of unconsciousness. It will be necessary to consider two types of unconsciousness: first, the unconscious of psychoanalysis, and, second, the unconsciousness of sleep and coma.

Generally speaking, psychoanalytic theory about the relation of the conscious to the unconscious follows the naïve view of evolution as a building-up process. It conceives the conscious

[1] Even supposing that it could be checked scientifically, the information so gained, being objective and mediate, would be subject to doubt.

simply as a late outcropping of the unconscious, and not as of a fundamental nature at all. But from the standpoint of metaphysic, the unconscious of psychoanalysis is that with which the conscious Self is so closely identified that it is not yet an *object* of consciousness. In practice, when psychoanalysis refers to 'the conscious' it is speaking of that area of psychic life *known* to consciousness; it is not speaking of the very power of consciousness. As we have seen, what consciousness knows objectively is precisely *not* consciousness itself.

Thus 'the conscious' is not consciousness; it is that area of psychic life with which the Self is no longer identified. The psychoanalytic unconscious consists, therefore, of (1) the as yet unrealized Self, which is as a matter of fact highly conscious, but not of itself as an object; and (2) an area of psychic life with which the Self (as the *buddhi*) has identified itself so closely that it does not recognize or know it objectively. This latter consists of various aspects of the soul which, when unconscious, are not experienced in their true form, but are projected outwardly in *symbolic* form.

Projection is the mechanism whereby we represent as outside the soul what we do not recognize as existing objectively within it. At the superficial level, we project upon other people motives and attitudes which we are unwilling to recognize in ourselves. At a deeper level, we project certain basic processes of the soul into dreams and myths, and into those universal mythological symbols which Jung calls 'archetypes'. At the deepest level, deeper than the soul itself, we project externally the very Self into the symbol of an objective and 'outside' God.[1]

There is some resemblance between psychoanalysis and the preliminary part of *yoga*. The first phase of *yoga* consists in distinguishing the Seer from the seen, the *via negativa* of realizing that the Self *is not* any known object. Likewise, psychoanalysis aims to know the unconscious objectively. It makes us aware that what we project is actually within ourselves, but the moment we recognize anything within ourselves, we have distinguished it from the knowing Self. The practical function of psychoanalysis is to heal the soul—that is, to get the *whole* psyche into consciousness. For while some part of the psyche is unconscious, that is, identified with the Self, it causes confused

---

[1] Of course, if God is infinite in the strict sense, the terms 'objective' and 'outside' are wholly inapplicable to him.

and unobjective reactions to life. For example, when we are unconscious of our own hostility, we project hostile motives upon others, and so fail to establish rapport with them.

Ordinarily, psychoanalysis does not plumb the unconscious deeply enough to reveal the Self and get it fully distinguished from the ego. However, Jung's analytical psychology does reach a point where this at least begins to take place, and he uses the very term 'the Self' for the new centre of psychic life which is found when the analysis reaches its culmination. But here analysis stops; it does not proceed, with *yoga*, to understand the identity of the Self with the infinite.

The aim of psychoanalysis has much in common with the aim of religion, that is, salvation or the saving of the soul. For the proper meaning of salvation (σωτηρία) is to make the soul whole, to rescue all its essential parts from the unconscious, from the dark underworld, from hell. The other side of the process, the realization of the identity of the Self and the infinite, is distinct from salvation, and does not come within the province of either psychoanalysis or religion.

The great obstacle to religious salvation is selfishness, that is, the unobjective type of action which results from the identification of the soul with the Self. To deny oneself is actually to deny that the soul is the Self, to cast out or to objectify the ego, and thereby distinguish it from the true identity, the *atma*. But because religion confuses the soul with the Self, it uses the phrase 'self-denial' instead of 'soul-denial'.[1] Of course, the ego can no more deny itself than one can jump out of one's own skin. The Self must deny, cast out, or objectify the ego—and thereby truly *love* and save it. Having, then, no concept of the Self, religion replaces it with the idea of external Grace, which 'comes in' from the 'outside' God.[2]

---

[1] However, cf. St. Luke xiv. 26: 'No man can be my disciple who hateth not . . . his own soul (τὴν ψυχὴν ἑαυτοῦ).' Also ix. 24: 'He that loseth his soul (ψυχὴν) for my sake, he shall save it.' Cf. Also St. John xii. 25.

[2] In concluding this section on the relation of metaphysical to psychoanalytical concepts, it is necessary to insert a note on Jung's theory of the structure of the soul. Jung gives the soul *four* functions—sensation, thinking, feeling, and intuition, and the process of psychic integration is complete when all four have been brought into consciousness. In discussing the soul we have mentioned only *three* of these functions—reason (thinking), feeling, and sensation. We have

We may now pass from the problem of the psychoanalytic unconscious to one that is more subtle, the problem of unconscious*ness*. What happens to the Self in deep, dreamless sleep? Does not the absence of any psycho-physical objects in this state simply prove that there is no consciousness apart from them, and that therefore consciousness is merely a function of the soul-body?

The Vedanta answers this problem by saying that in the state of deep sleep (*sushupti*) the Self 'reassumes' its original omniscience. There is no memory of this on waking for the simple reason that memory is a function of the soul-body, being, at it were, the traces of past impressions on the psycho-physical organism. The eternal Self needs no memory because it has no past. In eternal and omniscient consciousness past, present, and future are simultaneous, as previously explained, and for this reason events in time leave no trace upon the eternal consciousness. In sleep, then, time, which is the mode of knowing things successively, disappears, leaving alone and 'unclouded' the eternal mode of knowing proper to the Self. On the awakening of the soul-body, the Self focused upon it 're-enters' the successive way of knowing things, and as the omniscience enjoyed by the Self in sleep was never knowledge *for* the soul and the senses, no record or track thereof remains in memory.

The difficulty in understanding this point is that we generally confuse the Self with the memory, and the continuity of the memory with the eternal persistence [*sic*] of the Self behind the changing flux of experience. But the consciousness of the Self is strictly a *now*-consciousness, and it seems to remember the past only because the memory-traces on the psycho-physical organism are present. The Self can only be said to remember in the completely different sense of 'remembering itself', of 'reassuming' not a past but an eternal consciousness, of ceasing, as it were, to focus itself as the *buddhi* upon the particular and individual point of view.

done this to avoid any confusion between intuition, as a part of the soul, and the intellect or *buddhi*, which orientalists so often translate as 'intuition'. For Jung, intuition is not *buddhi* at all, but a sort of unconscious sensation. We believe that Jung's classification has much to recommend it, but its proper explanation would involve a considerable digression from our main theme. The reader is referred to his *Psychological Types* (Princeton, N.J., 1971), Vol. 6 in the *Collected Works of C. G. Jung*.

# THE SUPREME IDENTITY

## [iii]

We are now in a position to ask how and why the ultimate Reality takes points of view at all, why it identifies itself with beings like an actor simultaneously and effortlessly playing an indefinite number of parts. We saw in the previous chapter that the infinite has the power of abandoning itself to or identifying itself with the finite without the slightest loss of its infinite status. Similarly, a man of true rather than assumed dignity can play games with children without the least loss of dignity. We have seen, too, that because the infinite is absolute freedom, it is under no necessity to manifest the finite. Therefore we cannot answer the question *why* all this happens in terms of purpose, for purpose is a motivation found only in finite and temporal beings. To have purpose is to work for the attainment of a future goal determined by a present lack. Obviously, then, the infinite can have no purpose, for being infinite it lacks nothing, and being eternal does not live in terms of past, present, and future. Religion speaks of God as having a purpose only because it conceives him, analogically, in terms of time.

An action dictated by no necessity is likewise not work in the sense of labour. The Vedantists and Taoists say time after time that the infinite Reality does not *do* anything, though this is usually understood by Western commentators as meaning that the infinite is in a state of absolute inertia. But when it is said that the infinite does not *act* or *do*, this must be understood in the sense of *labour*; the infinite does not act under necessity or through effort. In scholastic language it is *actus purus*, pure act, because there is nothing potential in itself which it has to bring forth by effort or through the lapse of time.

An action both effortless and purposeless has its nearest human equivalent in *play*, for which reason Hindu tradition often refers to the *maya* of the finite universe as the *lila* or play of *Brahma*.[1] The same idea is implied in the following passage from Proverbs, describing the action of the Divine Wisdom or the creative agency of God:

[1] For the same idea in a Christian context, see my *Behold the Spirit* (New York, 1971), pp. 173–84.

# THE SUPREME IDENTITY

'I was his delight day after day,
playing in his presence constantly,
playing here and there over his world,
finding my delight in humankind.' [1]

The poetic idea of the universe as the play or dance of God reveals the meaning of the fact that all finite beings are transitory, constantly flowing and changing, that death is essential to finite life, and that in resisting change we are resisting the very principle that makes life lively. Though beyond all terms of duality, the infinite is life rather than inertia; it is the pleroma, the absolutely complete rather than the empty. If its total perfection is to be expressed in finite terms at all, only indefinite variety, multiplicity, and movement can afford the slightest approximation to its interior richness. The unceasing flow of life mirrors the boundless possibilities of omnipotence as well as the truth that the infinite, as *living* Reality, as spirit pure and simple, can never be grasped in any fixed form. Every form of life must become past; no form can ever take possession of the infinitesimal eternal Now, of the ever-present moment in which it is manifested. The Now remains; out of it and through it the forms of life flow with unbroken continuity, pausing not even for the most irreducible fraction of a second. Occupying neither space nor time, the eternal Now contains the whole universe; apart from it nothing has reality or life.

What we call the present moment is a function of consciousness. It is the eye of the Self, wherein the ultimate Reality takes the viewpoint of the infinitesimal rather than the infinite, though the two are in principle one.

'This is the Spirit that is in my heart, smaller than a grain of rice, or a grain of barley, or a grain of mustard-seed, or the kernel of a grain of canary-seed. This is the Spirit that is in my heart, greater than the earth, greater than the sky, greater than heaven itself, greater than all these worlds.' [2]

As absolute everywhere and everywhen the infinite is *Brahma*; as the absolute here and now it is the *atma*, the ultimate point of view, the Experiencer, the Witness, the Knower, in every life that is lived. Fundamentally, then, all joy and sorrow, all pleasure and pain, all love and anger, all enlightenment and

[1] Proverbs viii. 30-1. Trs. James Moffat.
[2] *Chandogya Upanishad*, III. 14. Trs. Juan Mascaro.

93

ignorance, are known by none other than the infinite Self, freely and deliberately abandoning itself to and identifying itself with every finite point of view. Transposed into religious terms, this is the Incarnate Son of God at the feast in Cana and on the Cross at Golgotha, participating in every extreme of human experience, the unique Incarnation having its metaphysical counterpart in the unique Knower of all knowledge.[1]

From the standpoint of the infinite as *Brahma* this universe is the instant, simultaneous and effortless manifestation of his own finite image. It will be obvious that because the total image is what the infinite 'wills', the infinite finds it absolutely 'acceptable', or, as we must say in human language, beautiful and good, since we term those things beautiful and good which accord with our will. But from the standpoint of the infinite as the Self, the *atma*, identified with a finite point of view, the manifestation of the universe is a gigantic work involving struggle, agony, trial and failure, the discipline of frustration, patience, and courage. These are the materials in which the image of eternal beauty is made—the exquisite Maya which mythology represents as the eternal Beloved of God.

'It is made of consciousness and mind; it is made of life and vision. It is made of the earth and the waters; it is made of air and space. It is made of light and darkness; it is made of desire and peace. It is made of anger and love; it is made of virtue and vice. It is made of all that is near; it is made of all that is afar. It is made of all.'[2]

---

[1] Cf. Coomaraswamy, *On the One and Only Transmigrant*, in Supplement to *Journal of the American Oriental Society*, vol. 64, No. 2, p. 40: 'Only, indeed, if we recognize that Christ and not "I" is our real Self and the only experient in every living being can we understand the words "I was an hungered . . . I was thirsty . . . Inasmuch as ye have done it unto one of the least of these my brethren, ye have done it unto Me." (Matt. xxvi. 35 f.)' This would bring out the deeper sense of Isaiah liii. 4: 'Surely he hath borne our griefs, and carried our sorrows.' Likewise, Galatians ii. 20: 'I am crucified with Christ, nevertheless I live; yet not I, but Christ liveth in me.' One who understands this knows that '*Ye* are dead, and your life is hid with Christ in God . . . who is our life.' (Colossians iii. 3-4.) 'No man hath ascended up to heaven, but he that came down from heaven, even the Son of man which is in heaven' (John iii. 13); therefore, 'Whither I go, *ye* cannot come' (John viii. 21), and hence, 'If any man would follow me, let him deny himself' (Mark viii. 24).

[2] *Brihadaranyaka Upanishad.* Trs. Juan Mascaro.

Thus in the ultimate fulfilment of the finite universe which the infinite knows and wills in eternity, no value is lost, no suffering is in vain, no evil remains untransformed, meaningless, and inane, to deny omnipotence with a co-eternal spirit of defiance and wrath.

Because the religious point of view conceives Reality as the One God rather than the non-dual infinite, the religious, and more especially the Christian, mind has a natural difficulty in accepting and understanding the doctrine of the Supreme Identity. The implication seems to be that the universe is after all only one thing playing at being many, which would appear to be both meaningless and immoral. For if this be true, there is no ultimate meaning (significant relationship between creature and Creator) and no ultimate value (distinction between good and evil); there is only barren, cold, senseless monism.

We must repeat again, and it cannot be stressed too often, that because the infinite is non-dual and not merely one, it does not exclude the realms of relationship and value. Relationships and values, though not eternal in themselves, do not ever pass out of the infinite consciousness, to which all that was, is, and shall be is eternally present. As a rod, which has a beginning and an end in space, endures through time, so things which have a beginning and an end in time are present in eternity. From the standpoint of time finite events are known successively; from the standpoint of eternity they are known simultaneously. Eternity is not a state of void and blankness which is all that is left when time comes to an end; to enter eternity is not to leave all the relationships and values of time in the past. The infinite and eternal includes time and space eternally, though not necessarily.[1]

But the religious mind shows its limitations when it attempts to regard relationships and values as *absolute*, as *of* eternity rather than *in* eternity. Being analogical, the religious point of view cannot be absolute, and involves the most serious contradictions when it tries to be so. Though the problem of good and evil will be discussed in the next chapter, it should be obvious that if the distinction between good and evil is to be made

---

[1] Cf. Guénon, *La Métaphysique orientale* (Paris, 1945), p. 17: 'He who cannot escape from the standpoint of temporal succession so as to see all things in their simultaneity is incapable of the least conception of the metaphysical order.'

absolute and eternal, it is completely impossible to escape absolute dualism. At this point, however, we are concerned only with the problem of meaning, of the religious impression that the doctrine of the infinite as the Self in man renders the universe no more than a meaningless shadow-play.

Meaning, as already indicated, is to be defined as significant relationship, as between lover and beloved, knower and known, subject and object. For the term 'meaning' is grammatic. A sentence has meaning only when it contains, actually or by implication, a subject and an object related by a verb. A monism is a subject without an object, or an object without a subject, that is to say, either pantheism or materialism.

It is not difficult to see that the religious point of view itself becomes meaningless when one tries to make it absolute. We intimated in the previous chapter that, pushed to its logical conclusion, pure monotheism becomes monism. If God is one, and if he existed before the universe was created, he was at that time related to nothing but himself—which is a strictly monistic and fictitious relationship. Out of this original oneness and absence of relations, it is impossible that there should ever have come multiplicity and relationships.

Christianity, however, does not think of God as merely uniform, but as One in Three—the eternal Father as the subject, the eternal Son as the object, and the eternal Holy Spirit as the verb—the lover, the beloved and the love. But if the fact that the Persons are really three and yet really one does not render God meaningless, then it must necessarily follow that the fact that selves are really many and yet really identical does not render the universe meaningless. One cannot have it both ways, stating that whereas unity in trinity makes God meaningful, unity in multiplicity makes the universe meaningless. If the One in Three God can be meaningful, then the One in Many (i.e. non-dual) infinite can be meaningful—and just as remote from monism.[1]

[1] In so far as the religious point of view is relative and not absolute, it is of the highest importance for it to insist on the meaningfulness of God. It is open to question, however, whether one should speak of absolute meaning, since meaning is relational and thus relative. The point of the above remarks, however, is to show that the metaphysical view of the infinite as One in Many has just as much, or as little, meaningfulness as the religious view of God as One in Three. Strictly speaking, the Absolute transcends meaning, and is meaning-

There is thus the closest analogy between the doctrine of the Trinity and the metaphysical doctrine of non-duality, an analogy which becomes still closer upon deeper inquiry. Underlying the three Persons, though not as a thing or object distinct from them, is the Godhead. In the non-dual being of the Godhead, the Father, the Son, and the Holy Spirit are three relations. Apart from the Son, the Father is not the Father; apart from the Father, the Son is not the Son; apart from the relationship between them, the Holy Spirit is not the Holy Spirit. The Son is said to be *begotten* of the Father, and the Holy Spirit is said to *proceed* from the Father and (or, through) the Son. However, the Father is the fountain-head (πηγή) of the Trinity according to the doctrine of the 'divine monarchy', and thus bears somewhat the same relationship to the Son as the infinite to the Self, as *Brahma* to *atma*. Like the Son, the Self is 'begotten not made, being of one substance with the Father', whereas the soul-body and the objects of the Self's knowledge are 'made'.

Because it altogether surpasses logical description the doctrine of the Trinity is the nearest thing in religion to a purely metaphysical doctrine, though in primitive Christianity it had not received a metaphysical expression. Indeed, the doctrine was not formulated at all fully until the Christian *religion* had begun to adapt itself to certain metaphysical concepts of the Neoplatonists. At the same time, the doctrine remains a religious doctrine in practice, because in practice the religious mind still regards God as One rather than non-dual. It remains, then, an analogy of the non-duality doctrine, and the one cannot be substituted for the other. They correspond, but are not equal.[1]

The main ground of the objection of the religious mind to the doctrine of the Supreme Identity of the Self and the infinite

*less* in the same sense that it is the No-thing, in the non-privative sense of metaphysical negation. It is possible, on the other hand, to say that the Absolute is meaningful in the sense that it has interior relations.

[1] Cf. St. Dionysius, *Theologia Mystica*, v. 'Neither is he Spirit, as we can understand it, nor Sonship, nor Fatherhood.' Also St. Thomas, *Summa Theol.*, I. Q. 28, a. 3: 'There must be real distinction in God, not, indeed, according to what is absolute—namely, essence, wherein there is supreme unity and simplicity—but according to that which is relative.' Also St. Augustine, *De Trinitate*, v. 5: 'Not all that is said of God is said of his substance, for we say some things relatively, as Father in respect of Son: but such things do not refer to the substance.'

is that love, the highest form of meaningful relationship, is impossible between man and God unless (a) the self of man is definitely and absolutely other than God, and (b) capable also of not loving him. But if this be true, it will also be meaningless and impossible for God the Son to love the Father, since both are God. Moreover, few theologians would be ready to admit that the Son could possibly *not* love the Father. If God is love essentially, then the Son, as God, will be love essentially.

It is, of course, obvious that the doctrines of the Trinity and of non-duality alike involve many logical difficulties simply because metaphysical principles are beyond the grasp of dualistic thinking. But the foregoing is intended to show merely that Christian doctrine cannot validly be used as an objection to metaphysical doctrine.

Finally, to ask what is the meaning of the entire process of the infinite manifesting itself as the finite, of ultimate Reality playing all these innumerable parts, is to ask the meaning of love, the meaning of relationship, the very meaning of meaning! The point of the infinite 'imagining' finitude, distinction, personality, and variety is precisely the point of finitude, distinction, personality, and variety, that is to say, of that very multiplicity of beings and relationships which the Christian theist so greatly values. It must be admitted, therefore, that any objection to the doctrine of the Supreme Identity on the ground that it takes out of life all the meaning which it has precisely manifested, and reduces all to a colourless monism, is without the least particle of validity. The further, and deeper, problem of whether it annihilates the values of good and evil, and renders the ultimate Reality an amoral monstrosity indifferent to suffering, sin, and evil is the subject of the next chapter.

# III. THE PROBLEM OF EVIL

## OUTLINE

1. The unsatisfactory state of the theological problem of evil is a symptom of Western man's unwillingness to be finite. His technological effort to make the finite infinite is in principle the same as his theological effort to make a relative position absolute.

Does the doctrine of the Supreme Identity abolish the distinction between good and evil, or does it actually solve the problem?

2. An examination of typical theological approaches to the problem shows that religion cannot make the distinction between good and evil absolute without falling into absolute dualism. But so long as there is no genuine realization of the Supreme Identity, the theological dualism must be maintained. The solution to the problem lies beyond theology, and must leave theology unchanged.

3. But if the ultimate Reality is non-dual, it does not invalidate or annihilate relative distinctions. To say that good and evil are relative is not to render them valueless distinctions.

Ultimately they must be regarded as mutually contributive to a single harmony—like light and shadow in a painting—a harmony of such superlative splendour that the dark involved in it, though still dark, is justified beyond all regret.

4. Does the idea of the necessity of evil (*O felix culpa!*) destroy the moral impulse? In theory there is certainly this danger, because any truth can be dangerous. But living experience of man's inescapable union with the infinite abolishes the fear, insecurity, and pride underlying all evil action. It makes it possible for him to accept rather than quarrel with finite limitations. This acceptance of limitations, coupled with a respect for the balance of nature, is the principle of true discipline.

Realization of the Supreme Identity manifests itself in unitive action (charity) as surely as the sense of ego and separateness manifests itself in separative and divisive action.

# III. THE PROBLEM OF EVIL

## [i]

The long history of theological and philosophical attempts to find a solution to the 'problem of evil' may well seem to make it a ground where angels fear to tread. For the finest minds of the Christian tradition have wrestled with it for generation after generation, leaving the answer much where it began—in mystery. But the problem, and by this we mean the way in which the Christian mind has posed the problem, has by now a sufficiently long history for us to observe and evaluate certain very practical consequences which the Christian attitude to evil has produced.

It has been noted that the traditional and spiritually unanimous culture of Christendom endured for a remarkably short time as compared with the traditional cultures of India and China, despite the fact that it had so much in common with them. At the present time many highly gifted minds are urging that we should return to the essential values and doctrines of this Christian culture, pointing out very justly and accurately the disastrous conditions which have come about through the relativism and empiricism of modern thought, through the wholesale abandonment of traditional standards. Yet such persons do not stop to ask why the medieval synthesis collapsed so easily, why it was not strong enough to withstand humanism and rationalism. They seem to see no historical connection between medieval and modern culture as between cause and effect, as between two opposite expressions of a single tendency which must alternate with one another so long as the tendency lasts. The peculiarly and, indeed, uniquely violent and disruptive character of modern civilization, the very emergence of a technology run mad, is not without roots in the medieval world. It has not appeared in Western culture out of a clear sky; it is not due to some uncaused act of folly or deviltry perpetrated by William of Occam, Galileo, Descartes or Luther. It is inherent in a certain peculiarity of the Western mind.

It is extremely difficult to trace the origin or judge the meaning of this peculiarity. Possibly it is not a peculiarity at all, but simply a natural phase in the development of certain races. The fact that we cannot find anything quite resembling it in other cultures may only be due to ignorance of history, for the first thousand or fifteen hundred years of Indian and Chinese culture, not to mention the early history of the oriental races, lie in the deepest obscurity. We should prefer, and shall try to show reason, to think that it is a natural phase, but we cannot be certain of this because comparable races are of such great and unknown antiquity.

This peculiarity is Western man's unwillingness to be finite, to accept the conditions of finite life. He seems to be by nature an uncompromising dualist or, which is to say the same thing, a monist—monism being the dualist's 'solution' of dualism. A dualist cannot accept the finite because he opposes it to the infinite; he cannot accept nature because he opposes it to God. He will therefore be compelled to resolve his dualism in one of two ways; he must either make the infinite finite, or the finite infinite; he must either force nature to be Godlike, or force God to be natural. While the attempt will have no effect on the infinite, it will either drag the finite to an altitude where it cannot breathe, or fill it with a value and a power which it cannot contain.

Such an attitude is natural to people who are extremely self-conscious, who are keenly aware of their own separateness from God on the one hand, or from the natural universe on the other. The sense of the isolation and loneliness of the ego is one of deep insecurity, manifesting itself in a hunger to possess the infinite. When he emerges from the primitive state, man loses that *participation mystique*, that identification of himself with his tribe and with the earth which Lévy-Brühl has noted as the dominant characteristic of primitive man. Feeling alone, feeling the impermanence, the weakness and the nakedness of his ego, this *parvenu* to culture and civilization must do everything possible to allay his insecurity, to drown his loneliness in the sense of infinitude. But just because of the exaggeration of the feeling of ego, the infinite seems to stand over against man as One wholly other, wholly opposite—everlasting as opposed to temporal, unchanging as opposed to changing, almighty as opposed to restricted, holy (the whole) as opposed to unholy (the isolated part).

Hand in hand with the experience of the lonely, insecure ego goes the sense of guilt. 'I am alone; I am free, but I feel unsafe. I feel exiled from my home. I must have done something wrong.' Man has eaten the fruit of self-knowledge, and has been expelled from the Eden of primitive unselfconsciousness. He has no longer any real assurance, for he has forgotten how to rely on his instincts, and must therefore plan his life with conscious deliberation. Thus every act, every step, is one of momentous consequence; everlasting salvation or damnation rest upon a single decision. The total impression of loneliness, insecurity, responsibility and guilt which accompanies the birth of self-consciousness is so intolerable that it must be escaped at all costs.

There are two ways of escape. One is to attribute the entire predicament to sin, to acknowledge the error of being an ego, and to beg the Infinite Other for mercy and restoration to the state of Eden. And then, as a mark of sincerity, the ego must in thought and deed renounce and denounce itself, and must embrace the discipline of perfection which will subject the nature of the finite and material to the laws of the infinite and spiritual. This is the 'Spiritual Combat' between the spirit and the flesh, presupposing the opposition of the two.

The other way is, instead of annihilating the finite in the infinite, to absorb the infinite into the finite. This will take the form of trying to make the finite infinite through technology, by abolishing the limitations of space, time, and pain. In terms of philosophy it involves giving the human ego the value of God.

Neither way is strictly and dogmatically Christian. For the central Christian dogma is the union of spirit and flesh in Christ. But the psychological attitude of both Graeco-Roman and mediaeval Christianity has been to regard the flesh as evil in spite of the dogma of the Incarnation and of the inherent goodness of all things created by God. In theory the fathers and the schoolmen accepted the goodness of the flesh, but in practice it was seen as an occasion of temptation, and the devil was symbolized as the purely animal aspect of man, as man with horns and cloven feet, the chthonic earth-god Pan.

It is easy, however, to over-simplify the medieval attitude to the finite, for the scholastic and patristic view of sin and evil was much more subtle than the popular identification of the devil with the flesh. The source of evil was regarded as the ego itself rather than its material vehicle. The thing to be denounced, denied and uprooted, the thing radically opposed to God, was the ego's own selfishness, the love of itself and its own property which stemmed from its sense of insecurity. But as such acutely self-aware persons as St. Augustine and Martin Luther observed, selfishness is inseparable from the ego; it is selfish by nature because it is born with the sense of insecurity. Man as ego is radically and originally sinful, and self-interest lies behind his loftiest acts of virtue. There was thus an opposition between God and the very centre of man's being. Restoration to fellowship with God would therefore depend on the annihilation of the ego's self-love, and its replacement by an out-going love of the purest generosity, a love which, since it is proper to God alone, could proceed from nothing other than divine grace.

In practice, however, this grace seemed a very rare gift, and if this was not to be attributed to arbitrary favouritism on the part of God, it must be attributed to a lack of that very virtue in the ego for which grace was so necessary. If, then, there was nothing that the ego could do to merit the gift of grace, and if the absence of grace was solely the fault of an ego which could do nothing to merit grace, the situation became intolerable. It was of no use to point out that in receiving the sacraments sufficient grace had actually and objectively been given, for the individual felt inwardly just as he had felt before. If he had received grace, he was not aware of it and thus unable to use it. If God is responsible for all the good in me, and I responsible for all the evil; if I by myself can do no good, and yet God's withholding of grace is my fault and not his—then the opposition between myself and God is ultimate. I am a lost soul; I am once again the lonely, insecure ego.

It was such a state of mind as this that really broke down the medieval synthesis. Sin and self-love in man were utterly opposed to God and must not be attributed to him. But without union with God, without grace, man has no power to avoid sin. So having no guarantee that God will give him grace, man is plunged into the sense of guilty insecurity from which he must escape. Thus he turns humanist, rationalist, agnostic, and atheist. If God will not give him the grace to escape from insecurity and sin, from fear and self-love, he will have to escape by himself. By the exercise of his own brilliant reason he will abolish the painful finitude of being an ego. He will forget his loneliness in crowded urban life, in an orgy of superfluous communication and social agitation; he will explain away his guilt and sin as the result of a wrong environment which technology, education and psychology will speedily correct; he will compensate for the sense of insecurity by proving himself lord and master of nature. But man is now faced with the fact that this solution, too, has broken down. The finite simply will not be made infinite, and the limitations which we have overcome in medicine, communication, industry and transportation come thundering back upon us in economic chaos and war.

In short, the medieval and the modern life-goals are essentially the same. The object in both is to possess God. In the former, the means are sacraments, penances, disciplines, prayers and formal virtues, by which it is hoped that God will be moved to enter the ego and displace its self-love. In the latter, the means are technological, and the hope is still that by such means man may acquire a Godlike power, mastering unruly nature by medicine, education and psychology. Both are self-contradictory. In the one, man is free to choose the good, but only by the grace of God—without which he is inevitably sinful. In the other man is free to rule nature, but at the same time his very reason is determined by naturalistic mechanisms.

Neither view of life accepts man's finitude. The medieval mind would not admit that self-love was the inevitable consequence of feeling insecure, which is in turn the inevitable result of the sense of ego. It thought, 'I ought to be like God; I ought not to feel insecure; I ought not to love myself. Therefore I am guilty.' It was therefore blind to the astonishing *pride* of the presupposition, 'I, a finite ego, ought to be like God', and it was in line with this pride to insist on man's possession of a free will so Godlike that, in the case of sin, it could act as a First Cause. Similarly modern man has the conceit that he *ought* to be able to master himself and nature by technological means. And because of this impossible *ought*, Western man medieval and modern is tormented by guilt.

The sense of guilt arises in an acute form in periods of breakdown, when some attempt to fulfil the compulsion to be like God has failed. At the close of the medieval period, Luther and Calvin denounced the Catholic 'optimism' that man was perfectible, that he could acquire merit by good works, and insisted on the doctrine of man's total depravity. At the close of the

# THE PROBLEM OF EVIL

modern period, Barth and Niebuhr denounce the optimism of the humanists, and lead the ponderous rumble of the so-called 'Back to Sin' movement in Protestantism.

Obviously the root of the trouble lies in the concept of sin, in the notion that some categorical imperative lies upon the human ego to be like God. But this is an extremely serious problem that admits of no easy solution. If we get rid of the notion of sin and free-will, if we saddle God with the responsibility for good and evil alike, if, in short, we deny that the ego is God's image, we seem to be faced with two dangers. The first is that man becomes nothing more than God's puppet, and God himself becomes arbitrary, amoral and cruel as the sole author of crime, war and tyranny. The second is that such an idea would undermine every moral impulse in man, and give him every excuse for an attitude of total irresponsibility. Have we not already seen the consequences of this kind of thinking in the results of the prevailing philosophies of determinism in our own day? Is not such a solution as this itself just another escape from the ego's overwhelming sense of loneliness, guilt and responsibility?

The time has come when this so-called problem of evil simply has to be faced. Despite all that was said and written about it, the medieval world did not face it. The 'Back to Sin' movement does not face it either, and if that movement is followed its course will be found merely circular. To restore the 'dignity' of the human ego, its Godlike freedom of will, its responsibility and its capacity to sin, is to precipitate once again the dilemma of Pelagianism versus Augustinianism. The Pelagian notion that man's nature is not so perverse as to be unable to do good without God's grace will be found as contrary to experience and to the Christian scriptures as ever. Only the most naïve persons will ever be able to believe that the ego can cure its own selfishness. Thus Augustinianism will again win the day, posing once more the insoluble problem of grace. The Semi-Pelagian compromise, that whereas man is not free to do good without grace he is yet free to accept or reject the offer of grace, is merely carrying the problem back one step—to a point where it remains essentially the same.

Before we can consider the light which the metaphysical viewpoint throws on this problem, we must consider it in more detail from the religious point of view. It will, perhaps, already be apparent that the root of the difficulty which religion finds in the problem is due to identifying the *imago Dei* with the ego rather than the Self, and that this in turn is more or less inevitable when there is confusion between the Self and the ego. But the religious mind will hardly be sympathetic to the intrusion of the metaphysical viewpoint until it is clear that strictly religious attempts to solve the problem are useless.

[ii]

Stated in religious terms, the problem of evil is approximately this:

1. If man can do no good without divine grace, and if such grace is offered to all, why is it that some accept the gift of grace and others do not? If the acceptance of grace is itself a good action, must not grace be necessary to perform it? If the latter question is answered affirmatively, will it not follow that God, by withholding grace, is responsible for man's refusal and thus for his persistence in evil?

2. It is answered that the fact that man can of himself do no good is not a circumstance for which God is responsible; it is the result of original sin, which may be traced either to the first selfconscious man or to some pre-mundane being, who, of his own free will, preferred himself to God. But what moved this being, whether man or angel, to prefer himself to God? If the act was unmoved and not the result of any defect in his God-given nature, the problem will arise as to whether it is possible for a finite being to be a prime mover, to perform a wholly uncaused and unmotivated act.

3. If it is allowed that man can, of his own power, accept or refuse the offer of grace, and that refusal does not result from any defect of nature which God has failed to remedy, the same problem arises as above: can man, would man, make an evil choice out of a clear sky, without any predisposing motive, without any pre-existing defect such as inculpable ignorance?

The problem as stated rests on certain presuppositions:

1. That it is unthinkable for God to perform an evil act or to be in any way responsible for anything more than the risk of its occurrence.

2. That such a risk is involved in the creation of finite beings other than God with the ability to love God. For to be able to love him, to give themselves to him of their own free volition,

they must be able also to refuse to love him, and to direct love to themselves instead.

In short, it is held impossible to love, in the highest sense, unless that love is purely voluntary. If God were to compel man to love him, such love would be as mechanical and insignificant as human love given under the influence of an aphrodisiac.

3. That the distinction between good and evil is absolute, since God—the ultimate Reality—is definitively good. If the distinction were not absolute, human acts would not be said to have any eternal and therefore real significance.

4. That God's foreknowledge or omniscience does not detract from the freedom of the created will. To know that man will sin is not to cause him to sin. If God were to refuse to create those whom he foreknows as sinners, this would amount to depriving man of the freedom to sin.

The crux of the problem, if the possibility of free-will be granted, is whether that freedom could be of such a kind as to refuse God despite sufficient knowledge of his glory, and despite the absence of any defect of nature. If, however, free-will is not granted, the problem is then to decide what is the function of evil in the divine scheme, and whether the ultimate significance of values can be maintained.

The great majority of Catholic theologians have held that evil is to be attributed solely to the free-will of the creature—at least originally. Even if this does not represent the actual truth, such an opinion is natural and indeed necessary in an epoch when man is experiencing the loneliness and isolation of his ego. It is possible that this experience is a necessary stage in the development of man's consciousness, and if so the belief in free-will will be as right and proper in that stage as it is right and proper for a child to take its 'make-believe' seriously. Once again, should the metaphysical viewpoint suggest a very different solution to the problem, it would not rule out Catholic theology as wrong. On the contrary, it would suggest that it was relatively right; relative, that is, to the contemporary state of man's consciousness. If it suggested that the religious viewpoint on this matter was not absolutely right, this would only be to say that a religious doctrine cannot in the nature of things be absolute. To try to make a religious doctrine absolute is to carry an analogy too far, and is another example of our attempt to make the finite infinite.

In view, however, of the collapse of both the medieval and the modern attempts to possess God, and of the violent crisis thrust upon the world by a civilization which would not accept finitude, it may well be possible that we are to witness the very gradual beginnings of a modification of Western man's consciousness. Such a modification is indeed fervently to be hoped for if mankind is to learn any lesson at all from present history, and it may be that the growing influence of oriental culture upon the Western world is a sign of its beginning. As already suggested, changes of this kind do not directly depend upon the deliberate adoption of a new point of view by vast numbers of people. In such matters the influence of a small persuasive minority is tremendous. It is not too much to hope that the course of events will move such a minority to realize that there is no essential opposition between man's finite consciousness and the infinite, and that the nature of the infinite is not to annihilate limitations but to love them.

The point which Western man has been unable to accept is that in the finite realm good cannot exist without evil. The Western free-will theory asserts that evil is a wholly unnecessary defect of finite and contingent being. Good may come out of it under the overruling providence of God, but it is unthinkable that God should have created a universe in which evil is a necessary element. Evil was therefore brought into the scheme of things on the sole responsibility of the created will.

It is important to understand the conditions under which a clear moral choice between the love of God and the love of oneself could take place. It is hard to imagine that man himself ever existed under such conditions, for which reason Catholic tradition takes the origin of evil back to the angelic realm, to the fall of Lucifer, the highest and most radiant of created spirits. This tradition has the great advantage of posing the moral problem in an extreme form, because it removes all grounds for finding the origin of evil in the necessary limitations of the human state.

The conditions under which a free and deliberate defiance of the divine will can be made are three:

1. To avoid the attribution of evil to ignorance, the created will must have a *sufficient* knowledge of God to make it perfectly clear that God is immeasurably greater than any other good, and that the choice of any lesser good as one's supreme love will have utterly disastrous consequences. In making Lucifer the

first sinner, Catholic theology leaves no doubt on this point. As the most radiant of angels he enjoyed an immediate consciousness of the divine glory, and clear understanding of what the rejection of that glory would entail.

2. To avoid the attribution of evil to some natural and inherent lack of power, the created will must be endowed with the capacity to love God.

3. For the same reason, the created will must be endowed with a rational nature, able to distinguish between its own good and its own evil, for otherwise the choice of self-love might be ascribed to congenital idiocy.

One is asked, then, to believe that under such conditions a created being conjured up out of nothing a malice so incredible as to doom himself and countless others to everlasting damnation. We say 'out of nothing' because there was nothing in his nature as God created it to make such an act necessary. The origin of the act lies solely in the freedom of the will to move in a direction to which absolutely nothing compels or moves it save, as St. Thomas always insists, what it conceives as its own good. But in this case there was no defect in Lucifer's knowledge of his own good; he was not labouring under misapprehension or doubt. He conceived self-love as his own good despite the certain and inescapable knowledge that it was not, and this may not be ascribed to any defect of rationality.

Granting that such an act was possible, however incredible it may seem, one cannot escape the impression that it is suspiciously like a First Cause, that in willing love to himself instead of to God, the choice of direction was an unmoved act. St. Thomas tries to escape this predicament by saying that the original mover in the act was God, for God moves all wills to the good, but that the deflection of the direction of movement was not of God and that therefore the act was not unmoved absolutely but only accidentally.

'God is the cause of every action, in so far as it is an action. But sin denotes a being and an action with a defect. But this defect is from a *created cause*, viz., free choice, as falling away from the order of the First Cause, viz., God. Consequently, this defect is not reduced to God as its cause, but to free choice; just as the defect of limping is reduced to a crooked leg as its cause, but not to the power of locomotion, which nevertheless causes whatever there is of movement in the limping. Accordingly,

God is the cause of the *act* of sin; and yet he is not the cause of sin, because he does not cause the act to have a defect.'[1]

What, then, is the cause of the defect in the action, of the crookedness of the leg which perverts the power of locomotion? St. Thomas answers that the created will is the cause. But why does the created will introduce the defect? Because, he answers, of a disorder called malice.

'Now the will is out of order when it loves more the lesser good. . . . When an inordinate will loves some temporal good, e.g. riches or pleasure, more than the order of reason or divine law, or divine charity . . . it follows that it is willing to suffer the loss of some spiritual good so that it may obtain possession of some temporal good. Now evil is merely the privation of some good, and so a man wishes knowingly a spiritual evil, which is evil absolutely, whereby he is deprived of a spiritual good, in order to possess a temporal good; and hence he is said to sin through certain malice, or on purpose, because he chooses evil knowingly.'[2]

This, however, is only to say that the will in question is so disordered that it will sacrifice the greatest good for the lesser. It does not explain the disorder. It does not show *how* the will gets so disordered that, by choosing a lesser good, it wishes knowingly an absolute evil. It must first disorder itself, and then, as a result of the disorder, be so incredibly stupid and malicious as to prefer the lesser good to the very greatest. But why should or would it disorder itself? To be able to prefer the lesser to the greatest? Such a wish implies disorder already. Why does it 'fall away from the order of the First Cause' (which is what 'disorder' means)? Does not such a falling away imply that a disorder of the will already exists, to make the falling away desirable?

At this point the problem revolves in a vicious circle. If it cannot be said that God disordered the will, then the will must have produced disorder in itself for no reason whatsoever. The will was originally in order; then out of an absolutely clear sky, it suddenly decides to be disordered—and through no inherent weakness for which God can be considered responsible. But St. Thomas insists that the will invariably acts for a good. Thus it will be absurd for an originally ordered will to consider disorder

---

[1] *Summa Theol.*, I-II. Q. 79, a. 2.
[2] *Summa Theol.*, I–II. Q. 78, a. 1.

a good; only an already disordered will could move in this way.

If, then, we rule out the possibility that the disorder comes from God, or from a defect of reason or appetite in the nature which God created and for which he would thus be responsible, we are left either with a total absurdity, or with the proposition that the original disordering of the will is itself a First Cause. In the midst of pure goodness, the principle of evil suddenly emerges from nowhere. Absurd as it may be to posit more than one First Cause, this is what the Thomist solution actually requires. Evil cannot be ascribed to absolute non-being, for this would have no power to produce defects in being of any kind, whether absolute or contingent. It must therefore be ascribed to a power uncaused by God, and this immediately presupposes the absurdity of an absolute dualism—a dualism already involved in a theology which can accept the necessary consequence of such absolute evil, namely an eternal hell opposed to an eternal heaven.

This impossible conclusion is the necessary result of trying to make the religious and especially the moral point of view absolute. But the religious mentality is afraid that if moral values are not absolute they are as good as annihilated. The reason for this fear is the error of opposing the absolute or infinite to the relative or finite, of thinking that at some time relative and finite things will be annihilated in the absolute and infinite.

If the theologian could admit that evil is strictly relative, and that there is no absolute evil (a proposition which St. Thomas, somewhat inconsistently, admits),[1] there should be no objection to saying that God is the creator of relative evil. For in the eyes of God relative evil would not be evil absolutely. In conjunction with relative goodness, like the conjunction of light and shadow in a painting, it could be said to serve and be necessary to some higher good which, like the beauty of the painting, would be predictable of the finite order in its entirety.

Such a view has, indeed been held by Christians and is clearly the view of many of the authors of the Bible.

'I am the Lord, and there is none else. I form the light, and create darkness; I make peace and create evil: I the Lord do all these things. . . . Woe unto him that striveth with his Maker!

[1] *Contra Gentiles*, III. xv.

Let the potsherd strive with the potsherds of the earth. Shall the clay say to him that fashioneth it, "What makest thou?".'[1]

St. Paul echoes the same thought:

'So then he has mercy upon whomever he wills, and he hardens the heart of whomever he wills. You may say to me then, "Why does he still find fault? For who can resist his will?" But who are you, a man, to answer back to God? Will what is molded say to its molder, "Why have you made me thus?" Has the potter no right over the clay, to make out of the same lump one vessel for beauty and another for menial use? What if God, desiring to show his wrath and to make known his power, has endured with much patience the vessels of wrath made for destruction, in order to make known the riches of his glory for the vessels of mercy, which he has prepared beforehand for glory.'[2]

But despite the liturgical admonition 'Remember, O man, that dust thou art, and unto dust thou shalt return', the Christian mind has never been able to accept the idea that man is mere inert clay in the hands of the divine potter. To give these passages from Deutero-Isaiah and St. Paul their full force would seem to make man no more than a puppet in the hands of a very arbitrary God, dispensing wrath and mercy according to mere whim. Such, indeed, is the God of Calvinism, to whom the Catholic consciousness can only react with horror.

If, then, we are to reject both the implied dualism of the Lucifer or free-will solution and the obvious injustice of the potter and clay solution, what remains? Let us ask, first, why it is that Christian sentiment reverts again and again to the notion that man is more than clay. The reason lies in that strange intuition of an eternal identity mentioned in the preceding chapter. But while this identity is confused with the ego, the human soul-body, and while freedom of will is therefore associated with that ego, the problem must remain unsolved. As soon, however, as it becomes clear that the centre of man's being is not the ego but the Self, and that the Self is the incarnation, the deliberate self-limitation of the infinite, it will be seen that the potter and clay theory involves no injustice at all. For in this circumstance, the conscious spirit in the vessels who experiences wrath and mercy is ultimately he who dispenses them.

[1] Isaiah xlv. 7, 9.
[2] Romans, ix. 18-23.

It will follow, then, that our intuition of free-will is derived in principle from the fact that the Self is one with the infinite freedom, that our will is in the last resort identical with the infinite will. If this makes the possibility of real love between man and God a mere empty figure of speech, the doctrine of the Trinity will, as shown, collapse for the same reason. The love of God the Son for God the Father would have to be an empty figure likewise.

The fallacy in the theological presuppositions about the problem of evil is that man cannot be said to love God unless he does so of his own volition. For as a matter of fact, when we experience great love we experience it as a compulsion; we adore those whom we cannot but adore. Yet the action of love is not simply mechanical. The element of freedom in love which always remains to our intuition is due to the fact that the love with which we love is God's. We have no love of our own, as egos, to give God. We love him with his own love, as mirrors turned to the sun reflect its light.

'As long as man loves something else than God, or outside God, he is not free, because he has not love. Therefore there is no inner freedom which does not manifest itself in works of love. . . . As God can only be seen by his own light, so he can only be loved by his own love.'[1]

Indeed, it is God's own love that moves in us even when we are unaware that God himself is its proper object.

'Human love, in spite of all its ignorance, blindness and even downright error, is never anything but a finite participation in God's own love for Himself. . . . Even in the midst of the lowest pleasures, the most abandoned voluptuary is still seeking God; nay more, as far as regards what is positive in his acts, that is to say in all that makes them an analogue of the true love, it is God Himself who, in him and for him, seeks Himself.'[2]

## [iii]

The horror of evil as we experience it, even if it is only relative, makes the religious mind recoil from the thought that it can be God's will. But the necessary consequences of the theory that

[1] *Meister Eckhart's Sermons.* Trs. Claud Field, pp. 54 and 57.
[2] Etienne Gilson, *The Spirit of Mediaeval Philosophy* (London and New York, 1940), p. 274.

evil originates in the free-will of angel or man is literally one of infinite, or more correctly, everlasting horror. To envisage a God who can permit a world-order involving even the possibility of the everlasting hell is surely more profoundly immoral than the idea of a God who can cause relative evil. Nothing is more immoral than absolute moralism.

On the other hand, if evil is relative, and if the consciousness which experiences it is an incarnation of the eternal being, it is possible to construct a theory of the finite universe which really makes sense. If such a theory can be held, no sin, no agony in the entire history of the universe will be without its eternal and positive significance. Though the effects of such a view upon the moral impulse have yet to be considered, a theory of the universe such as we have in mind would be far more congenial to the moral sense than either the free-will or the potter and clay 'solutions'.

In the previous chapter it was suggested that the finite universe is, in the consciousness of the infinite, the instant, simultaneous and effortless manifestations of its own 'image'. Considered as the all embracing, the ground and cause of subject and object, and of all relationship, the infinite finds its supreme finite analogy in love. Now love involves two elements or movements —a movement of separation, and a movement of union, an element of frustration, and an element of satisfaction. If love is to be manifested at all, that is to say, if there is to be any finite expression of love whatsoever, it is impossible that lover and beloved be identical in the sense of simply one. If I am my beloved, I have no one to love. To love there must be union with the beloved, but also separation. For love is a creative tension; it is like the string of a musical instrument—a single string yet pulled in opposite directions. If there is too little tension, or if there is too much so that the string breaks, it will give forth no sound. The perfection of love is like the perfect tuning of the string, for love attains its fulfilment as there is the maximum of union between two beings who remain definitely separate. Unity in duality is the law of the finite.

In principle the infinite is unity, but finite unity cannot be manifested without duality. In principle the infinite is life and being, but finite life and being cannot be manifested without death and non-being. In principle the infinite is consciousness, but finite consciousness cannot be manifested without unconsciousness. In principle the infinite is light and goodness, but finite light and goodness cannot be manifested without darkness and evil. It is not to be understood that there is anything imperfect or regrettable in this necessary polarity. On the contrary, from the eternal standpoint these oppositions are seen as harmony, the dark side ever enhancing the beauty of the light. Death renders life more lively; darkness makes light stand out more brilliantly; separation makes the union of love more intense; suffering and evil are the essential media of courage and repentance, perfecting the splendour of goodness.

From the successive standpoint of the Self in time the harmony is unseen. The pairs of opposites alternate and consciousness would hold to the light and annihilate the dark. But from the simultaneous standpoint of the Self in eternity the light and dark colours blend into a harmony whose total effect is so much more splendid than light, or life, or goodness known simply by themselves in the successive order, that the utterly incomparable beauty of the vision makes the most hideous evil experienced in time infinitely worth while. If, then, the incarnate Self in each one of us is, in the fullness of time, to awaken to a vision of the entire finite order of such splendour that the worst evils will be transformed into instruments of beauty, we may judge some small fraction of the vision's glory from the very depth of those present evils which it will so much more than amply repay.

In our present state of consciousness we are standing, as it were, with our eyes right against the painting, so that only one small, meaningless patch of colour can be seen at a time. But in our eternal state we stand with the whole canvas in view. From this standpoint evil is not evil as we now know it; it is shadow harmonizing with light. We can only guess dimly at the perfection of artistry that is needed to harmonize such shadows, such intensities of blackness, as the squalor and depravity of our cities, the tortures of concentration camps, the ugly hypocrisy of the self-righteous, and the piteous suffering of the diseased, the deformed and the insane. No one can presume to condemn those who, having experienced such things, are so moved with repulsion that they can only call upon God for the everlasting damnation of those responsible for them. Thoughtless as such a judgement may be, the human mind *in extremis* cannot be expected to think in accord with the infinite understanding of God. Who will be so bold as to denounce a very human thoughtlessness when even the saints (most of whom have known suffering and evil to the roots) have felt sin to deserve such a punishment?

This view of the function of evil in the finite order is, however, profoundly consistent with such truly fundamental Christian dogmas as the Incarnation and the Holy Trinity. The God-man Christ on the cross is without doubt our most eloquent religious analogy of the infinite as the experiencer of all human pain and evil. And if the universe is a finite image of the Trinity, it must express, in the successive order of time, both the union of the Son with the Father and the distinction of the Son from the Father—the latter as the fall of man from God in Adam, and the former as the union of man with God in Christ, the Second Adam. It throws light, too, on the great 'dark saying' of Jesus, 'It needs be that offences must come, but woe to that man by whom the offence cometh', a saying that calls to mind the problematic rôle of Judas, whose betrayal of his Master precipitated the Redemptive Sacrifice. Already the Church has expressed a hint of this insight in the strange words of the Paschal Praeconium sung at the blessing of the candle on Holy Saturday:

'It availed us nothing to be born, unless it had availed us to be redeemed. O how admirable is thy goodness towards us! O how inestimable is thy love! Thou hast delivered up thy Son to redeem a slave. O truly necessary sin of Adam, which the death of Christ has blotted out! O happy fault, that merited such and so great a Redeemer.'

As might be expected, so great a mind as St. Thomas was by no means entirely blind to such a principle.

'There are in the world many good things which would have no place unless there were evils. Thus there would be no patience of the righteous, if there were no ill-will of the persecutors; nor would there be any place for a vindicating justice, were there no crimes; and even in the physical order there would be no generation of one thing, unless there were corruption of another. Consequently, if evil were entirely excluded from the universe by the divine providence, it would be necessary to lessen the great number of good things. This ought not to be, since good is more powerful in goodness than evil is in malice.' And again:

'If evil were taken away from certain parts of the universe, the perfection of the universe would be much diminished, since its beauty results from the ordered unity of good and evil things, seeing that evil arises from the failure of good, and yet certain goods are occasioned from those very evils through the providence of the governour, even as the silent pause gives sweetness to the chant.'[1]

According, then, to the doctrine of the Supreme Identity, the values of good and evil are not abolished on the one hand nor made absolute on the other. Both are seen as relative to a superior harmony, and evil is understood as the separative movement of love as experienced from the limited standpoint of succession and time. Goodness, which in this scheme is just as necessary as evil, is the manifestation in time of the unitive movement of love. It finds its supreme archetype in Christ, as the separative movement finds its archetype in Adam or Lucifer, who, in the Old Testament, is almost invariably the personification of the 'dark side' or the wrath of God. Terrible as the separative movement may appear to be from the temporal viewpoint, the realization of the Supreme Identity makes it possible to say with St. Paul, 'I reckon that the sufferings of this present time are not worthy to be compared with the glory which shall be revealed to us.'[2] In the light of eternal vision that which is called evil from the standpoint of time is seen in its proper context as an essential element of a harmony more perfect than any amount of temporal good, such that it is said of God, 'Thou art of purer eyes than to behold evil, and canst not look on iniquity'.[3]

It is, perhaps, all too easy to see the fallacy of St. Thomas's account of the origin of evil; it attempts a rationalistic solution of the problem, and, as Berdyaev has so clearly shown in his *Freedom and the Spirit*, in any rationalistic view of the spiritual world freedom is already excluded. To Berdyaev, however, the idea that evil is a moment in the manifestation of a greater good, appearing as evil only because of the finitude of man's knowledge, is also a rationalism. It would seem to deprive man, as man, of any real freedom, and leave only the freedom of God. Berdyaev insists that a distinct human freedom in which evil has its origin must be preserved. His treatment of the problem is probably the most profound in all theological literature, but at root it remains unsatisfactory.

[1] *Contra Gentiles*, III. lxxi.
[2] Romans viii. 18.
[3] Habakkuk i. 13.

For Berdyaev, as for the Christian mind in general, there can be no significant relation between man and God which is not free on both sides, and where there is not an ontological distinction between the two. While he has seen that pure monotheism is substantially monism, and that the significance of God can only be vindicated by the doctrine of the Trinity, he does not apply the logic of the relations between the Persons of the Trinity to the relation between God and man. If man and God cannot have a true relation without the ontological distinction, and without a freedom of man distinct from the freedom of God, it must follow that a true and significant relation is impossible between the Persons of the Trinity.

'The mystery of the unity between two persons finds its solution in the Trinity. . . . The kingdom of Love in freedom is the kingdom of the Trinity. The experience of freedom and its inherent tragedy bring us to the Trinity. . . . Absolute monotheism is always despotic, for it regards God as an absolute monarch and leaves no place for freedom. Only the religion of God in Three Persons succeeds in definitely getting past this monarchist or imperialist conception of God by revealing the life of God as a divine Trinity and thus vindicating liberty.'[1]

But if the idea of the Trinity vindicates liberty within God, if the fact that the Father, the Son and the Holy Spirit are all God does not deprive them of significance and freedom, there is likewise no deprivation if man's Self and the infinite, *atma* and *Brahma*, are also distinct and yet one. For the same reason, as has been shown, there is also no monarchist or imperialist tyranny of God over the human puppet.

To account for the origin of evil Berdyaev comes extraordinarily close to the metaphysical position by seeking it in a primordial freedom, a state of infinite possibility beyond good and evil, from which all the manifestations of life proceed. This primordial freedom lies at the very foundation of man's inner being.

'The possibility of evil is latent in that mysterious principle of being in which every sort of possibility lies concealed. The void (the *Ungrund* of Boehme) is not evil, it is the source of every kind of life and every actualization of being. It conceals within itself the possibility both of evil and of good. An initial, irrational,

[1] *Freedom and the Spirit* (London, 1935), p. 139.

118

and mysterious void lies at the heart of the whole life of the universe, but it is a mystery beyond the reach of logic.'[1]

Because Berdyaev does not identify this primordial 'void' with God, nor even see the religious idea of God as its analogy, it is really impossible for him to escape from the anomaly of finding the origin of good and evil alike in a principle *prior to* God. His attempt to avoid this anomaly is ingenious, but radically unsatisfactory.

'In the beginning was the Logos, the Word, the Meaning, and the Light. But this eternal truth of religious revelation only means that the kingdom of light and meaning has been realized initially in being and that the Logos triumphed from the beginning over darkness of every kind. Divine life is a tragedy. Even at the beginning, before the formation of the world, there was the irrational void of freedom which had to be illuminated by the Logos. This freedom is not a form of being which existed side by side with the Divine Being, the Logos, or Mind. It is rather that principle without which being could have no meaning for God, and which alone justifies the divine plan of the world. God created the world out of nothing, but it would be equally true to say that he created it out of freedom.'[2]

The inevitable consequence of seeking the origin of evil apart from or prior to God is to deprive him of his infinity, to make his life *dependent* on some other principle distinct from him and necessary to him.

'Creation must be grounded upon that limitless freedom which existed in the void before the world appeared. Without freedom creation has no value for God. In the beginning was the Word, but in the beginning also there was freedom. The latter is not opposed to the Word, for without it the Meaning of the Word does not exist. Without darkness there is no light. Good is revealed and triumphs through the ordeal of evil. Freedom makes both good and evil possible.'[3]

In spite of himself, Berdyaev is admitting that the evil is necessary to the finite manifestation of the good, and thereby subordinating it willy-nilly to the higher good, to the absolute good, of God's creative activity in which, as he is forced to admit, it is a necessary element. 'Without darkness there is no light.'

[1] Ibid., p. 165.
[2] Ibid., p. 165.
[3] Ibid., pp. 165-6.

Then if the light be splendid enough, the darkness is justified. And if the darkness is justified, there is no compulsion to separate the primordial freedom in which it originates from God. The void of primordial freedom is God's own infinite nature.

Now this answer to the problem is not, as Berdyaev supposes, a mere rationalism. To show that evil is necessary is not to subject the entire realm of being to necessity, nor to attempt to make absolutely everything susceptible of a reasonable explanation. There is a point at which explanation comes to a full stop, a point beyond which lies only the mystery of the divine being. No possible reason can be found for the emergence of anything at all from the infinite freedom. Likewise, no reason can be found for the fact that evil is necessarily subordinate to a higher good; it is conceivable that good might have been necessarily subordinate to a higher evil. For these two ultimate mysteries, these two wholly unnecessary acts of divine freedom, we can only offer the most profound thanks. They are sufficient by themselves to vindicate both the freedom and the love of God.

We must be careful, however, to keep religious and metaphysical concepts distinct. The religious idea of God presupposes the identification of man with his ego, and so long as man feels himself to be the ego and no more, it is necessary and almost inevitable that he relate himself to God as one free and independent being to another. This situation becomes problematic when we try to make it absolute for the simple reason that it is not the absolute situation. However, the religious viewpoint is not and cannot be absolute, and therefore we can advocate no change in religious doctrine about the problem of evil. So long as man feels himself to be the ego, to deprive him of freedom (or the sense of freedom) is to subject him to the despair of being a mere pawn of the divine tyrant. Furthermore, this very sense of freedom is what will ultimately lead him to the discovery that he is more than ego.

Indeed, Berdyaev's insistence that man's being has its ground in the same primordial freedom which is essential to the creative activity of God is precisely an intuition of the Supreme Identity. In metaphysic the God-man polarity of religion is transcended but not annihilated, because the non-duality of Supreme Identity is sympathetic to and inclusive of all distinctions. But religion cannot understand the metaphysical position as other than monism. It cannot understand a realization of identity with the infinite as anything other than a denial of man, of man's freedom, and of all significant relationship. Yet because it transcends the God-man polarity, the Supreme Identity cannot be said to take away man's freedom and leave only God's; the freedom of the Self is just as much man's as God's; it is the one freedom, the one ground, underlying and making possible all relationship whatsoever. But for this common ground, man and God could never be related, just as without their common Godhead, Father and Son could never love each other.

This whole discussion of the theoretical difficulties of theological solutions to the problem of evil is not intended, as we have said, to advocate any change of doctrine. The point is simply that the theological and religious viewpoint should begin to accept its own relativity, and to admit the possibility of a realization wherein the dualism of creator and creature is transcended, a level of knowledge and being at which the problem of evil disappears. Hard as this may be for a point of view which can only see monism in such a transcendence of dualism, the fact remains that the longer religion attempts to hold an absolute position, and to be a substitute for metaphysical knowledge, the more untenable, embarrassing, and discredited that position will become.

## [iv]

'Shall we then sin, that grace may abound?' All that has been said raises this old, practical problem, which is the real reason why the religious mind is so afraid of any Doctrine of Supreme Identity or of the absolute and universal supremacy of the divine will. If men believe that all evil is from God, that our very sins are his will, and that in the last resort they can only contribute to the glory of a superior good, will they not be profoundly demoralized? It seems that no sanctions at all remain for discipline and self-control, no grounds for personal responsibility, no urge to repentance and moral effort.

Understood in a merely superficial and theoretical way, there is no doubt at all that the view set forth has this danger. But the fact that it is dangerous is no proof that it is untrue. Atomic energy is excessively dangerous, but it exists. Very wisely religion has in the past kept this 'mystery of iniquity' under the ban of serious heresy. It would be hard, however, to imagine Western civilization in any more serious danger than that which now threatens it as a result of refusal to accept the finite limitations of man. Dangerous predicaments need dangerous remedies, and the thing from which Western man needs above all to be delivered from in his present plight is fear. Fear of one another, fear of war, fear of death, judgment and hell, fear of the loneliness of the ego, has made us victims of a sense of vertigo. Fascinated by the precipice on whose edge we stand, we are drawn irresistibly to end our dread by taking the jump. Fear makes the trigger finger nervous, and the ultimate irrationality of atomic war will come upon us neither through hate nor desire for empire, but from fear that the other side will begin first.

Neither is atomic war our only danger. In every aspect of life Western civilization is deeply demoralized by loss of faith, by utter absence of any metaphysical certainty. Our cult of the passing moment, our vicious little escapes, our sexual opiates, our narcotic addiction to speed and agitation, all these are to drown out the fear of futility, of the plausible and all-pervading belief that the lonely ego faces only the inanity of ultimate extinction. Rumble and bombinate as the moralists may, all the prophecies of God's everlasting judgment and doom serve only to aggravate the suppressed terror in which we live.

Deterministic as our view may be, it has nothing in common with the determinism of futility, the notion that life is simply a machine in which we are helpless and wholly temporary cogs.[1] Optimistic as it may be, it has nothing in common with the vacuous optimism of the nineteenth century which looked for the abolition of evil in *time* as the result of inevitable progress—for an earthly paradise to be enjoyed by our posterity long after we ourselves had vanished for ever into dust. In the face of disaster neither of these views has the slightest power over fear.

During ten centuries the doctrine of the ego's cosmic responsibility, of its Godlike freedom to decide its own eternal destiny in a single act, has paralysed Western man with selfconsciousness. To escape from it he has had to deny the possibility of any

[1] But in fact this is determinism only from the strictly relative standpoint of the ego. Properly, determinism is the total subjection of man's life to Fate, to the will of an 'external' God, to a mechanistic world-order, or to the effects of past causes. But from the standpoint of the Self, there is no Fate, external God, past cause, etc., which determines it. The Self is self-determining, and only appears to be determined when identified with the ego.

eternal destiny at all, only to run into the despair of mechanistic naturalism. It is very simple for the absolute moralists to strike heroic attitudes and condemn the doctrine of Supreme Identity, as yet another escape from man's eternal responsibility, as the final dose of morphia for a hopelessly incurable moral disease. The more self-righteous and provincial type of occidental is ever apt to associate all that comes out of Asia with opium, exoticism, *laissez-faire*, and moral turpitude, as if cultures given to such things could endure for more than three thousand years and were to be judged *in toto* by symptoms which they manifest in their extreme old age. It is surely the mark of the most serious spiritual insensitivity not to be able to distinguish the weakness of old age from its wisdom. Mature judgment will rather see a positively providential blessing in the fact that the metaphysical doctrines of the Vedanta are made available to us in the time of our most urgent need.

Admitting, then, that this view of the problem of evil is dangerous as mere theory, though not as dangerous as it might be under present circumstances, it must be remembered that it originates not in speculation but in realization. One may point to many persons who have held it either as knowledge or as overmastering conviction, and under such circumstances it has been anything but a pretext for moral dissolution.

'A man who from outside all religious experience reflects upon the probable effect of any vitally held faith is almost certain to reach wrong conclusions. He tends to suppose that anyone, who is convinced that God controls all things absolutely and without reserve, will feel himself relieved of responsibility and will adopt the attitude of "wait and see". But the man to whom divine control is not the major premise of a dialectical process but a dominating fact of intimate experience does not in this way settle down inertly to watch the activity of that control; the consciousness of control is itself an overmastering impulse, urging him to incredible enterprises and impossible endeavours. . . . To feel God's hand upon one impelling and directing, and to find oneself actively pursuing some course or serving some cause, are not two experiences but one. The doctrine of the universal Sovereignty of the divine will is paralysing so long as it is doctrine only; but when it is matter of personal experience, it becomes impulse and energy and inspiration.'[1]

[1] William Temple, *Nature, Man and God* (London, 1940), pp. 380-1.

What, after all, are the immediate causes that move us to immoral or evil action? Most obvious is the sense of *insecurity*, for it is from fear of the obliteration of the ego that we snatch greedily at pleasure while we may, that we steal, cheat, lie, murder and evade reality. Less obvious but no less important is the sense of *pride*. Now pride is associated with selfconsciousness, and has its origin precisely in the sense of the ego having free-will. Pride is on the one hand glorying in achievements that we attribute to our own power. On the other hand, the cancer of pride is no less at work in the guilty shame and self-pity of failure, the embarrassment of the ego in discovering that it is human after all despite the conviction that it ought to have behaved as if it were God. A third cause is possibly mere *inertia*. The excessive desire for rest and sleep is in all probability an escape, reducible to the sense of insecurity. In some cases it may be due to defective glands. A certain amount of inertia is simply natural and proper, and Western man of the Northern Temperate Zone could perhaps do with more of it to keep him out of meddlesomeness and agitation. His excessive activism is largely due to his cold climate.

It will follow, then, that if man knows or is convinced that his identity, his central Self, is one with the Infinite and eternal Self, and that all that he is and does as an ego is the will and action of the eternal Self, both insecurity and pride will tend to vanish. If he is certainly eternal, certainly united with God, what becomes of the urge to snatch greedily at life during its passage? Why should there be any excessive fear of pain and death, prompting him to injurious escapes and acts of violence? When every good that he achieves and that others achieve is known certainly to be the common work of God, where is the ground for pride? When he fails in the face of others' success, why should he be afflicted with hurt pride and envy, knowing or believing certainly that there is but one ultimate Enjoyer of failure and success alike? From the negative point of view, realization of the Supreme Identity cuts at the very roots of evil conduct.

Furthermore, neither realization nor theory does away with the fact that such evils as are clearly contrary to nature have the ordinary deterrent of unpleasant effects. If we are not free to avoid such evils, neither are we free to escape their natural penalties. If such deterrents do not affect the motives of the believer in predestination, they are of no more effect upon the believer in free-will.

A careful consideration of what realization involves will show that it offers no escape from responsibility for evil, even though this responsibility is of a different kind than theology supposes. One can attempt to shift responsibility by blaming the past, or fate, or God. But in realization it is found that there is no one and nowhere outside the Self whither blame can be shifted; realizing the Supreme Identity of the Self and the infinite, *atma* and *Brahma*, it is seen that there is nothing apart from the Self to be made responsible.

'The Self is the Lord of self; who else could be the Lord? . . . Evil is done by the Self alone; by the Self alone is one stained; by the Self alone is evil left undone; by the Self alone one is purified.'[1]

In short, one cannot shift responsibility to God when the polarity of God and man has been transcended.

'A man becomes liberated even in this life when he knows that God is the Doer of all things. . . . Not even a leaf moves except by God's will. Where is man's free will? All are under God's will. Therefore I say, "O Mother, I am the machine and Thou art the Operator; I am the chariot and Thou art the Driver. I move as Thou movest me; I do as Thou makest me do".'[2]

But this does not change the fact that if there is one will, which is both God's and mine, in so far as it is mine I cannot escape the consequences both physical and moral of its action. If I fall off a cliff *by mistake*, I am not absolved from death because there was no conscious intention of falling. If I hate another person wilfully, I cannot escape the moral consequence of being a victim of the fear and grief which hatred involves. In other words, the fact that we sin because of ignorance does not avoid the consequences, the bearing of the responsibility, of sin. Because of geographical ignorance, I fall off a cliff. Because of ignorance of the Supreme Identity, I hate another. In either event I must take the appropriate type of consequence, since the fact that I am in a state of ignorance and finitude at all is ultimately the will of that Self which is my own true identity. Is it then possible for justice to distinguish between the crime

---

[1] *Dhammapada*, 160 and 165.
[2] *Ramakrishna: Prophet of the New India.* Trs. Swami Nikhilananda. (New York, 1948), p. 107.

of a responsible person and the crime of a blameless lunatic? The distinction is fundamentally not of degrees of blameworthiness, but of different types of ignorance. The highest justice forgives both alike, but the very act of loving and forgiving requires that in each instance an appropriate medicine be given to cure the respective types of ignorance. The office of a judge is not to blame, but to judge, or diagnose, the type of ignorance and to prescribe the remedy. 'Condemn not, that you be not condemned. For with what condemnation you condemn, you shall be condemned; and with the rule by which you measure, you shall be measured.' For who judges the Self in another judges his own Self.

Thus far, however, we have only described the negative effect of realization. Obviously, it is not enough that our basic pride and insecurity be eliminated, for the body naturally withdraws from pain and nature in general prefers the course of least resistance. What is there to show that such realization would not produce a merely flabby, harmless and ineffective attitude to life?

First let it be said that mere nature is also active. A healthy body takes joy in exercise, and for reasons quite unconnected with anxiety or pride every soul likes to express itself. Were this not so, it would be difficult to see how the natural universe could exist at all. In any event, the mere pangs of hunger compel the body to find food and thus to work. But the positive effect of realization does not rely on any such naturalism, as if man would be 'naturally good' were certain obstacles removed.

Underlying the fear of the 'religious' objection to this entire point of view is a very profound absence of faith in God. One who realizes the Supreme Identity, who unreservedly admits that he, as the Self, is one with the infinite, thereby admits into himself that grace or power of the infinite which moves the unitive, as distinct from the separative, aspect of the universe. The fearful soul simply does not trust the supreme Self to supply this power. It is afraid that if evil is admitted to be necessary, it will somehow follow that good is unnecessary. While there is obviously no *logical* proof or certainty of the following truth, since creation cannot logically and necessarily be connected with the infinite, the fact remains that he who realizes the Supreme Identity is filled with a peculiar power of creative joy. Spiritual security issues in self-abandonment to work conceived as a kind of play, and executed with a particular sureness and lightness of touch.[1]

It should hardly be necessary to point to the extraordinarily disciplined lives and to the personal kindness and charity of almost every soul that has enjoyed profound mystical or meta-physical insight, whether occidental or oriental, or to the peace and joy wherewith their very presence has illumined others as a gift more precious than bread or gold. For a life lived in the realization of the Supreme Identity is as necessarily a life of unity as a life lived in the consciousness of ego and separateness is necessarily a life of conflict. Once the identification of the Self with the ego has been 'seen through' the separative or evil life is utterly inappropriate, and its powerful motivations wither away. Once the identification of the Self with the infinite is realized, the unitive or good life receives still more powerful motivations of its own, for God and the human race are known most vividly as a single family sharing a single 'blood' or life. The truth that 'inasmuch as ye have done it unto one of the least of these my brethren, ye have done it unto Me' becomes the central reality of experience. The divine power no more manifests separative action through the spiritually awakened than it permits a flower to grow with its blossom in the mud and its roots in the air. But he who would realize and be awakened must take the risk of receiving this truth without the slightest prior guarantee. The grace of God cannot be compelled. Whoever is afraid that realization will make the good life as unnecessary as the evil life is necessary is simply not ready for realization. Such a person must in the nature of things continue to believe and act on the hypothesis of individual free-will.

As already indicated, the intuition of free-will which all of us possess prior to realization is due to the identification of the Self with the ego. The Self is indeed free in so far as it is one with the infinite, but before realization its freedom as well as its conscious-

---

[1] Westerners will often point to the supposed absence of creative results from oriental spirituality. Such 'absence' is largely due, however, to the Westerner's lack of perception. He recognizes creative power only when it interferes in the course of nature with more or less violence. He is in general insensitive to the oriental idea of crea-tion, which consists in getting behind nature and pushing, examples of which are to be seen in Chinese painting and Japanese architec-ture. The oriental mind has the deepest respect for that *balance of nature* which we have so profoundly upset in agriculture, in industry, in animal husbandry, in medicine, and in the social order.

ness are assimilated to the ego-soul. Thus what the infinite wills is imagined to be willed by the ego. But as in religious terminology true freedom lies only in the abandonment of one's own will to the will of God, so from the metaphysical standpoint it lies in the clear knowledge that the will of the Self is principially one with the will of the ultimate Reality, and thus with its infinite freedom.

Paradoxically, it is only through realization of the Supreme Identity that man really accepts his own finitude. So long as man identifies himself with the ego he is trying to be God. It is only when he knows that his centre of being is the infinite that he is really free to be man, for we have seen that it is in the very nature of the infinite to accept, include and abandon itself to the finite. This is the reason why the most spiritual people are the most human people. They are natural and easy in manner; they give themselves no airs; they interest themselves in ordinary everyday matters, and are not for ever talking and thinking *about* religion. For them there is no difference between spirituality and usual life, and to their awakened insight the lives of the most humdrum and earth-bound people are as much in harmony with the infinite as their own.

This acceptance of their own finitude is the principle of law and discipline. For the discipline of the soul and body, and thus of the social order and its natural environment, is based on the proper love of finite things. To love the finite is to want to develop it in accordance with its limitations. There is no thought that such discipline is a means to 'attain' the infinite or to manifest a more perfect harmony with the divine nature. Things are to be loved because God loves them, because every single one of them comes into being through the self-abandonment of the infinite.

Modern man has little grasp of such discipline. In religion he will control his finite life in order to possess God. He perverts the whole idea of doing a work for God's sake, for his greater glory, by separating the glory of God from the actual doing of the work, making it a sort of ulterior motive beyond the work itself. But God is glorified, not when we conceitedly imagine that he stands in need of our service, but when we share his own love of the people and the things he creates. In industry, technology and the pursuit of pleasure modern man controls and 'loves' finite things, making them serve his hunger for infinitude.

But he does not really love matter and people and things; he loves the sensations, the intimations of omnipotence, which they can be made to produce when their proper limitations are violated. In his hunger for infinitude, material resources—forests, vast areas of soil, mineral deposits, animal and human bodies—are exploited and wasted with about as much reverence for matter as might be expected from a swarm of locusts.

Law and discipline based on reverence for limitations and love of the finite is an art that admits of no easy description or formulation. It is, perhaps, the very nature of art itself. For where does one draw the line that determines the proper limitations of a substance or a living body? At what precise point does use become exploitation? Just how far may the artist use a given medium without violating its character? To what exact stage may artificiality be employed to modify the balance of nature? What, above all, are the just limits of human nature within which man may remain without trying to be God?

Such matters depend to so large an extent upon sensibility rather than logic that no exact lines can be drawn. The essential principle, however, is that proper limits are exceeded at the point where sensibility turns into sensationalism, where the finite threatens to become infinite. The sign that the border has been crossed is when man takes to an enterprise like a drug, when he begins to expect his mind, his body or his tools to achieve more and more and more. To continue to give stimulation, the dosage of a drug must be increased. But to continue to give pleasure, a symphony does not have to be played louder and faster at each performance.

The psychology of 'bigger and better', of the record smasher, the money maker, the imperialist, the speed maniac, the time saver, and the religious fanatic is the psychology of the drug addict. He has not the faintest idea of when or where to stop. He knows only that he wants more and more and more of the same—more speed, more cash, more power, more territory, more converts, more thrills. He wants to possess infinity, whereas the man of sensibility asks only to be possessed by infinity. Thus in the certainty of his given and eternal identity with the ultimate Reality, man is at last free to love things and people for themselves rather than for what he can get out of them. Free from anxiety and impatience he can concentrate on the creation of quality rather than quantity. Free from the compulsion to deserve eternal life by piling up merits, he can love people with their benefit in mind rather than his own salvation. Free from the craving to possess spirit and life, he can devote himself to the perfection of form and matter.

Order, beauty and discipline, harmony and co-operation, exist already in nature below the human level. But the infinite Reality expresses itself as man to introduce a yet more complex and exquisite order. When man considers himself separate from the infinite, he manifests a chaos parallel to the necessary element of chaos in nature. Yearning for the infinite, he wrecks the finite limitations that seem to bar its attainment, first spiritually and then physically. But when he realizes that he is after all one with the infinite from the beginning, he is in a position to be a creative instrument and to fulfil the positive aspect of his destiny.

# IV. INVOLUTION AND EVOLUTION

## OUTLINE

1. The highest positive expression of metaphysical Reality is religious and mythological symbolism, which is interior and spiritual truth projected or extraverted into the forms of phantasy and fact. Prior to any metaphysical knowledge, we have no direct consciousness of interior truth, and can know it only as it is clothed in external forms.

But such forms show us only what metaphysical Reality *is like* in terms of the human mind; they do not show us what it *is* in itself. Failing to emphasize this distinction, modern Christianity has confused both itself and the contemporary world as to the proper use and meaning of religious terms.

The fact that the Christ-story is a projection and a symbol is not inconsistent with its historicity, although the Western mind has given this a disproportionate value. Although metaphysic penetrates this symbolism and transcends theological and historical forms, this does not make it destructive of dogma, nor a source of religious individualism.

2. The infinite Reality manifests itself as finite beings in two phases—temporal and successive expressions of an eternal and simultaneous polarity, analogous to the eternal union and distinction of God the Father and God the Son. These are:

(a) *Involution*, wherein the Self identifies itself with the separate ego, expressing distinction.

(b) *Evolution*, wherein the Self 'recollects' its own true nature, expressing union.

This evolution is not an *escape* from finitude, because eternity and the eternal viewpoint do not annihilate the reality of temporal experience.

3. The relation of Christian dogma and symbolism to the involution and evolution of the Self under the archetypes of Adam and Christ. Adam stands for a 'dark incarnation' which religion, as such, cannot and should not recognize. Raising the problem of a *gnosis* beyond religion, and the relation of *gnosis* to divine charity.

*The eternal viewpoint does not annihilate the reality of temporal exp.*

# IV. INVOLUTION AND EVOLUTION

## [i]

The story of 'lost and found', of death and resurrection, of self-forgetting and self-discovery, is perhaps the most common theme of mythological and religious symbolism. In one way or another the story of the Fall and the Redemption, the parable of the Prodigal Son, the symbols of the Zodiac, the mystery of Voluntary Sacrifice, and the innumerable myths of exile and return, tell of that primal and cosmological game of hide-and-seek whereby the finite universe is created. For this theme is the basic principle of all story, all adventure, all love, all meaning, because every aspect of life is an image in miniature of the central drama underlying the whole—the self-abandonment and the self-realization of the ultimate and infinite Reality in the finite order. For this reason Coomaraswamy has said that 'myth embodies the nearest approach to absolute truth that can be stated in words'.[1]

But in the twentieth-century mythology speaks almost a dead language, for the modern mind knows of no order of truth higher than historical fact. Myth is therefore rejected, and in place of its vivid and eloquent expression of metaphysical Reality we are compelled to substitute a cumbersome philosophical verbiage. Yet this substitution may not be in vain if, by means of it, some key may be given to the inexhaustibly fruitful and suggestive language of myth, which, short of metaphysical realization itself, embodies the highest understanding of the eternal principles. For the negative language of metaphysical doctrine is not really an *ex*pression at all; it is rather a cracking of the shells of mythical forms in order that their inner and inexpressible content may be known. But where there are no shells there can be no cracking, and no revelation of the inner content.

In discussing the relations between the infinite and the finite, we saw that if we did not 'personalize' the infinite we ran the

---

[1] *Hinduism and Buddhism* (New York, 1943), p. 33.

danger of conceiving it in a sub-human way—as an impersonal force like electricity, or even as a mere nothingness. We pointed out that the negative language of metaphysic must be understood, not as a privation of the infinite, but as an affirmation of its freedom from and superiority to every human conception. Yet the fact remains that if we are to talk and think about the infinite at all, if we are to have any positive symbol of it whatsoever, the symbol of the personal God is the most accurate and adequate—provided we recognize that it is only a symbol, and that the Reality exceeds our power of positive conception altogether.

But the Western mind has run into difficulty with religious and mythological language because it has taken these symbolical expressions of the inexpressible as statements of objective fact. Religion is saying simply that man's highest positive idea of God must be a human idea, but we have mistaken this for the statement that God *is* a person. In manifesting the human being the infinite is indeed acting like, or imagining itself to be, a person, and therefore the way in which it manifests the human mind will determine the way in which it symbolizes itself in the human mind. Light passing through a prism will be modified by the nature of the prism. But to say, for example, that, when translated into human thought, God is *like* a Father is *not* to say that God in himself *is* a male parent.

However, modern man is not entirely to blame for this misunderstanding, for he has taken the Christian religion at the valuation of its own exponents, who, more particularly in modern times, have so confused 'is like' statements with 'is' statements that widespread misunderstanding is only to be expected.

Something must first be said about the way in which religious and mythological symbols are formed. We have seen that the human being is manifested through the voluntary 'identification' of the infinite Self with a finite soul-body. In this act, the Self becomes correspondingly unconscious of its real identity, somewhat as the actor on the stage deliberately forgets himself through absorption in the part which he is playing. In making this identification, the Self becomes unconscious, not only of its own identity, but also of certain elements in the soul-body with which it is identified. It becomes so 'involved' with them that it does not see them. Just as the eyes, for example, are in the human face, it is for that reason harder to see one's face than one's feet.

Now it is a principle of psychology that what is unconscious internally is projected externally. A hidden light, shining from within, falls upon the 'screen' of the external world and *seems* to be shining from behind that screen. For this reason, mythological symbolism places the divine 'outside', and more especially out beyond the sky, beyond the furthest reach of consciousness, in the firmament of heaven. Thus the inner light of the Self and its immediate relations with the soul is reflected on, or clothed with, sensible images, whether these be material objects of a 'numinous' character, or phantasies and dreams.

In religious language this process of exterior projection is called the operation of the Holy Spirit, who *inspires* (breathes from within) man with divine revelations. But the interior meaning of these revelations is not necessarily known to the person who receives them, just as an artist who is inspired to paint a picture may reveal therein things about his own unconscious depths which he had no conscious intention of showing. For example, the author of the *Apocalypse* may have had the conscious intention of representing certain prophecies about the immediate future, or about a literal 'last day' in which God would come to judge the world. But anyone who can read the language of myth will see at once that the Holy Spirit gave the author far more than he may himself have realized, and that the *Apocalypse* speaks most eloquently of things that belong to the internal and metaphysical order.

The process of projection will account for the fact that the myths of all ages and peoples have certain basic elements in common, despite their superficial differences. For in them the one Self, the one Eternal Word or Truth, is making itself incarnate, or projecting itself, into the exterior world of variety and multiplicity.

The key, then, to the interpretation of myths is simply to 'introvert' them, on the understanding that they are the outward and visible signs of an inward and spiritual Reality, which, if it is to be formulated at all, must be represented as external simply because forms themselves are external. But the modern mind does not approach mythology in this way. It fixes itself upon the problem of whether or not myths are objective and historical facts, and, if not, upon what the originators of such myths may have had the conscious intention of representing. This is a singularly unprofitable line of inquiry.

But it is the historical result of a certain emphasis in post-medieval Christianity, which has tended to stress the factuality of the Christ-story above its interior sense, and to determine what is 'pure' Christianity by trying to discover the conscious intentions of the original apostles. This peculiar emphasis is justified on the grounds that symbolical' interpretations of the Christ-story are 'anti-historical' and fail to give historical reality the importance it deserves, since it is in history that the 'mighty acts of God' actually take place. This point of view involves such a complex interweaving of truth and misunderstanding that, before we can go on to consider the Christ-story from the interior viewpoint, it deserves some special consideration.

It has already been stated quite plainly that there is no conceivable conflict between metaphysic and Christian dogma, because dogma, without the slightest alteration, is a perfect analogy of realization. There is no conflict between dogma and and the metaphysical doctrine of the Self, because the former has absolutely nothing to say about the Self as such. In religious terminology man is the ego, and the ego is as principially other than God as it is other than the Self. Likewise, religion comprises no dogmatic definition whatsoever of the nature of consciousness.

But the Christian mind has the sense that the idea of God, and more particularly the historic Incarnation of the Son in Jesus of Nazareth, is something more than analogy or symbol. The latter was a real event in the time series, comprising the actual birth of Jesus from a virgin and his actual bodily resurrection and ascension after death. This insistence upon actuality and historicity gives the Christian symbols a unique character, which, as the Church maintains, must make them symbols of extraordinary importance to the whole world. It must carry the implication that Jesus was no mere symbol of what every man is essentially, but that no other historic individual is quite like him. He is unique on the plane of historical eventuality, and it is essential that this uniqueness be recognized. As a historical character, he is related to God in a way that no other individual ever was or is.

We do not think that the metaphysical viewpoint interferes

135

with these claims in the least. Let it be said first that metaphysic is not science, and therefore cannot regard virgin birth or physical resurrection as outside the bounds of infinite possibility. Nor is it at all beyond the bounds of such possibility that one should come into the world in whom there is no confusion of the Self with the soul-body, and who therefore never conceives himself as an ego or human individual. This is indeed precisely what Catholic doctrine says of Christ, that the Self (the divine Person and nature) is united with the human nature 'without confusion, change, division, or separation, the distinction of natures being by no means destroyed by their union'.[1] Furthermore, the Church insists that Christ is not a human person, even though he has a complete human nature, and this is simply to say, again, that in him the Self (the Person or *Purusha*) is not so confused with the human nature as to produce the state of ego-consciousness, of human individuality.

But all this is precisely the oriental doctrine of the Avatars, or incarnations of the personal God, of the coming into the world of certain men who are not individual because they do not confuse Self and soul. But Christians have never been prepared to admit this doctrinal similarity, because they insist that Jesus of Nazareth is the *only* real Avatar or Incarnation of God, and because the normal confusion of Self and soul gives the impression that the Self, the Person of God the Son, is not present in all men alike.

Yet what does Catholic dogma actually say? It certainly says that Christ is unique in so far as he is divine. He is the '*only*-begotten Son of God', but this expression refers to the uniqueness of the One who is incarnate, not to the uniqueness of the incarnation. Hindu doctrine will likewise insist that he who is incarnate as this or that Avatar is the 'One and Only', the sole real Knower or Self. Oddly enough, the conciliar formularies of Christian dogma say nowhere that Jesus of Nazareth is the only historic incarnation of God! They say that the Name of Jesus is the only Name whereby men may be saved, but, as is well known, the Name means the Spirit of Jesus, the Divine Son who is his Person. They say that the incarnation in Jesus is the means of salvation for 'the world' or 'all the world', but the term *world*, used in several senses in the New Testament, is not defined. If it should happen that *world* or *saeculum* or even *cosmos*

[1] Denzinger, *Enchiridion*, n. 148.

should be the equivalent of the Sanskrit *yuga* (epoch, age, order, cycle), the parallel with the Avatar doctrine would be complete. For Hindu teachings state that there is an Avatar appropriate to each *yuga*, each world-order or world-cycle, a period whose temporal and geographical limits are not specifically defined.[1]

The Avatar differs from ordinary men in that he is one in whom realization of the Self is 'born' rather than 'attained', and this in itself would suffice to make the historical Jesus in some sense unique. However, the idea that Jesus is unique in history, and stands at the Head of the human race, or of the Church as his Mystical Body, has also an important correspondence with metaphysical principle. For as Jesus is the unique Head of the Body, the Self is the unique centre of man considered as the psycho-physical body, but we must point out again that this 'introversion' of the idea of Christ as Head of the Body could hardly come within the sphere of dogmatic religion, since dogmas, as positive forms, belong necessarily to the external order. Thus religious dogma defines man only in so far as he is knowable, objective, and external; in so far, indeed, as he is *not* the Self. There is, furthermore, a correspondence between metaphysic and the very insistence of the Church on the historicity of Christ, and on the physical reality of his resurrection and ascension. The point here is not only that physical life is no obstacle to realization, but also that from the standpoint of eternal consciousness the physical world is not left behind (in the tomb), but known simultaneously in its state of wholeness and glory.

The fact remains, however, that from the metaphysical standpoint the *principal* importance of the Christ-story lies in its mythological character, that is, in what it incarnates or projects of that spiritual and interior realm which lies below the level of ordinary consciousness. Moreover, from this standpoint there will be no objection to the claim that the Christ-story is *both* mythological *and* factual, since it is obviously possible for concrete events to be myths, that is, for the Self to be projected symbolically not only into phantasy but also into fact.

Objections to the Christian claims may indeed be raised on purely historical and scientific grounds, but there are none at

[1] Needless to say, the 'world' in the minds of Hebrew and Hellenistic writers would be the then known world, bordering around the Mediterranean.

all on metaphysical grounds, and it is apparent that neither historians nor scientists can produce one shred of proof that the life of Christ *could not* have been lived as tradition records it. The most they can say is that the story is highly improbable, which is to say much less than the Church father, Tertullian, who called it 'absurd'. But there is nothing to prove that the improbable cannot happen.

However, the actual historicity of these events is of such importance to the Christian mind, that it will want to be assured not only that the metaphysical viewpoint tolerates their historicity but actually supports it—for 'he who is not with us is against us'. In the last resort Christianity judges a man by asking whether he is prepared to give his life to support the *historical* truth of the Incarnation, and all the miraculous events involved in it. It feels that he has no true understanding of God's nature unless he can stake his life on the belief that God has had the power, the love, and the respect for historical fact and value to make the Incarnation a truth of matter as well as a truth of spirit. The Christian mind feels that a merely mythological resurrection would be a symbol lacking integrity, lacking that concrete realization necessary to make it a complete and unique symbol worthy of the power of God. For concrete realization is the test of true achievement. The thing is not just an intention, not just a dream, not just an impalpable idea. It moved intractable matter. It rolled away a stone, and raised a body from the dead.

Now that modern thought has had ample opportunity to recover from the naïve scientism of the nineteenth century, it should surely be obvious that there is nothing to prevent us, either in reason or in feeling, in science or in morals, from accepting the historic Incarnation. But the historicity of the Incarnation will almost certainly become a secondary issue. For there is a peculiar significance in the fact that our Western and Christian culture has laid so tremendous and central an emphasis on Christ as historical miracle. For if the sure sign and seal of God's unique handiwork be made miracle, we are submitting him to the same test upon which scientism bases its own grandiose claims—that it does such sensational things with matter. It is not, after all, surprising that the culture which has made so great an issue of miracle is the culture which produced technology.

# INVOLUTION AND EVOLUTION

We believe in technology because it 'gets things done', by which we mean that it abolishes finite limitations. We admire men of action who leave behind the most startling physical achievements. We make the test of faith in God, nay more, the very test of God's own Incarnation among us, centre in a sign of special power over matter. Ultimately, then, it is not the beauty of character, not the profound significance of the story as symbol, not the wisdom, the love and the utter sincerity of Jesus which mark him as the unique Incarnation of God; it is the concrete achievement of rising from the dead. Upon this element of miracle our Christian culture has, with certain exceptions, fixed itself with such a peculiar passion and anxiety that whoever makes it secondary is felt to be denying it.

Primary emphasis on miracle and history is, however, a passing phase of Christian culture. It played a very secondary part in medieval theology. Such an emphasis is, at the same time, entirely appropriate to the ego-conscious stage of development, because at this stage the necessary task is the attempt to master one's finite limitations and compel nature by violence to submit to the pattern of God. In this stage death, old age and material frustration are necessarily viewed as evil, as contrary in principle to the divine will, and thus victory over physical death will appeal as the sign *par excellence* of the personal presence of God. It might well be argued that the Incarnation included physical resurrection for the precise purpose of making it intelligible to an ego-conscious humanity.

But modern man is ceasing to see any great spiritual import in miracle—and by 'modern man' we mean the leadership of contemporary thought. He is sympathetic enough to psychic phenomena and the possibility of transforming the material by mental powers. But by degrees he is learning to hunger for something more than technology, whether religious or scientific. There are signs of a dawning desire to prefer the knowledge of God to a resurrected body. To be sure, the majority is still estranged from Christianity by the anti-miraculous scientism of the last century, and now worships at the altar of science's own and more tangible miracles. It may indeed be that the majority will remain ego-conscious and miracle-minded for an indefinitely long period, but it is far better that they reverence a miracle with true analogy to the metaphysical order than one with none.

# INVOLUTION AND EVOLUTION

Unquestionably the majority will be deeply influenced by a strong intellectual leadership. Thus a revivified Christianity is not at all out of the question if the leadership can be found. But it will not be found so long as the element of history and miracle is made primary, and the element of metaphysical analogy almost wholly disregarded. Needless to say, the moral rather than miraculous emphasis of liberal Protestantism will prove even less effective. It is therefore of the highest importance that the modern mind be made aware of the fact that Catholic and traditional Christianity is *principally* significant not so much as history but as symbol, and as a symbol not merely of moral virtues but of metaphysical Reality that may be actually known.

Metaphysical traditions have always taken the miraculous in their stride, accepting it but never making an issue of it. For all his works of power, Jesus never indulged in miracles for their their own sake, and never let them become a test of truth. He reverenced the material order most deeply, but yet advised his disciples not to lay up treasure upon earth. One reason why missionaries find it so hard to convert so many of the more spiritual orientals is that they do not regard the miraculous as the most important sign of the divine agency. They accept Christ as an Avatar or Bodhisattva with the greatest ease, but, to the exasperation of missionaries, no amount of insistence on the historicity of the virgin birth and resurrection will make them acknowledge him as unique. Christ will seem unique to the oriental mind only if it can be made certain that his life and death, his resurrection and ascension, constitute the supreme analogy of metaphysical realization.

It must be obvious, however, that the presence of realization will diminish the importance of its analogies and symbols because they will cease to be the highest possible way of knowing the infinite, while remaining the best way of expressing it concretely. They will become instruments rather than sources of knowledge. Religion looks with a natural anxiety upon any way of knowing the ultimate Reality which transcends its own. It fears that such knowledge would tend to destroy the need for religion, to make its highly valued symbolism unnecessary and obsolete. It fears, too, a possible spiritual confusion resulting from the fact that realization is supposed to be a 'personal and private' experience which, unchecked by objective standards of dogma, might issue in the wildest religious individualism.

Both fears are groundless. For as long as man is a creature of reason, feeling and sense, symbolic analogies of the infinite will be necessary, at least as means of communication. And since it appears that at any given time only relatively few persons are capable of realization, analogy will remain the *only* source of knowledge for the majority. Nothing could be further from the metaphysical standpoint than a desire to overthrow religious analogy, to create any sort of sect or movement for the abolition and disuse of symbols, whether doctrinal, moral or sacramental. Such movements have existed, but have nothing in common with metaphysic. On the contrary, they represent a monistic, Manichaean, spiritualistic philosophy without the least comprehension of non-duality.

Ineffable as it may be, there is nothing 'private' about metaphysical realization since it is the Self and not the ego which realizes. The Self is no more the private property of any individual than the solar system, however much it may seem to be so while under the limitations of ego-consciousness. This is the reason why the various types of metaphysical doctrine are always in essential agreement whereas, conversely, systems of religious doctrine contradict one another. Individualism is the invariable result of cutting religion loose from its metaphysical ground, so that opinion, sentiment and personal preference run wild and can be kept in check only by an external and legal authority appealing to fear. Metaphysical realization never has been and never will be the source of religious individualism, representing as it does the world's only unanimous tradition. The type of 'mysticism' responsible for such individualism will invariably be of either the monistic variety on the one hand or, on the other, the visionary kind in which persons suppose themselves to have received specific revelations which, being symbolic in form, must on no account be confused with realization.

The fact that misinterpretations of various oriental doctrines have been espoused by religious individualists in the West who claim to find in them support for their own liberalism or modernism has created much confusion. Much of the Neo-Buddhism and Neo-Hinduism in vogue among Western dilettanti is nothing more than rationalism and sentimentalism dressed up in misapplied Sanskrit terminology. Nor has this confusion been clarified by the majority of academic orientalists who, translating original texts from the philological standpoint, have persisted in trying to identify Hindu and Buddhist doctrines with purely speculative concepts of Western 'metaphysics' with which they have little in common. Traditional Catholic Christianity is the Western world's nearest point of contact with a true metaphysic, that is, in so far as its doctrinal and sacramental structure is concerned. Its politics are another matter.

[ii]

From the successive standpoint of time, the drama of creation and redemption, of the infinite manifesting itself in the finite, may be divided into two stages. The first is involution, wherein the supreme Self deliberately forgets and lays aside its omniscience, and identifies itself with finite points of view—culminating in the experience of total separateness and independence as the human ego. The second is evolution, wherein the Self awakens to its true identity *within* the finite order, not forsaking it as a prison but using it as an instrument of expression.

That this process may be understandable to finite thought, the supreme Self must be regarded under two aspects. To one aspect, both phases are simultaneous because the eternal and omniscient viewpoint is never actually lost; the infinite remains infinite however much it may identify itself with the finite. To the other aspect the phases are successive, because, while remaining infinite, the Self becomes voluntarily subject to space and time. These two aspects are analogous to the Father and the Son in the doctrine of the Trinity. The first phase, involution, manifests in finite form the Son's distinction from the Father; the second, evolution, manifests his union with the Father. The infinite, in the act of manifesting and identifying itself with the finite, is the formative *logos*, God the Son, whose image is the entire finite order considered simultaneously, *sub specie aeternitatis*.

Although we speak of the infinite as having two aspects, one in eternity and the other in time and space, one omniscient and the other taking finite viewpoints, this is simply a concession to the inherent dualism of human thought. In reality the infinite remains undivided, but the idea of the double aspect is a symbol for its non-duality, its ability to be at once infinite and finite, itself and another, one and many, without the slightest contradiction.[1]

From a slightly different point of view these two principal phases, involution and evolution, may be considered as three: the unconscious, the ego-conscious and the Self-conscious.[2] In the first, the Self is so wholly absorbed in the process of self-abandonment that it is not aware of its own identity, or of the subjective side of knowledge, in any important degree at all. In the second, it has begun to be aware of itself, but is confused with the more central objects in its point of view, that is to say, with the psycho-physical complex of the human ego. In the third, it is aware of itself as distinct from the ego, and one in principle with the infinite. However, in this third stage the finite viewpoint is not completely relinquished and omniscience reassumed, because the significance of entering the finite state is not simply to enter and leave, but to express the infinite in finite terms. The movement of involution ends and evolution begins in the middle of the ego-conscious stage.

The period of unconsciousness may also be considered as the stage of unconscious *union* of infinite and finite, a union which cannot be made conscious unless followed by a period of conscious division. To learn to appreciate his home, the Prodigal Son had to be separated from it, to travel into the loneliness and dereliction of a far country. Similarly, the Self emerges into consciousness as the separate and lonely ego, for by this means it 'comes to itself' like the Son in the parable, and begins the journey back to conscious union with the Father. Once again, however, the finite viewpoint is not abandoned because the

[1] Most of the great Christological problems which baffle theology are the result of the mind's difficulty in understanding non-duality. If Christ is the God-man, how can the omniscience proper to him as God co-exist with the finite consciousness proper to him as man? Will not the former simply obliterate the latter? The problem has never had a satisfactory theological solution because it is essentially a metaphysical problem, resolvable only in metaphysical terms. To the extent that theology must remain in the analogical sphere of religion, the problem must lie beyond its legitimate scope.

[2] The term 'unconscious' includes both unconsciousness proper and that type of unselfconsciousness so absorbed in the contemplation of objects that it does not think of itself. The term 'ego-consciousness' denotes what is popularly called selfconsciousness in the 'awkward' sense of the word.

object of the journey is conscious union of the infinite *and the finite*.

'The accompanying diagram (Figure 2) is appended to show the cycle of involution and evolution, together with the three stages of the unconscious, the ego-conscious and the Self-conscious. The basic form is, of course, a circle—the traditional finite symbol of eternity. From the eternal viewpoint the circle exists instantaneously, but in order to describe a circle in time, one must begin at some starting point, go *away* from it and then return to it. The original division of the two points of the compass, one at the centre and the other at the circumference, is the

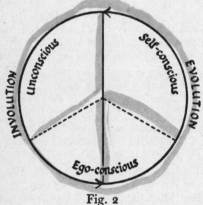

Fig. 2

primal 'creative division' of *Brahma* and *atma*, Father and Son.

Nearly every mythology looks back to a Golden Age from which man has fallen. From one point of view this Golden Age may be regarded as the state of the Self before it 'fell' into the self-imposed limitations of finitude, though the 'fall of the divine nature into matter' must not be considered, in the Manichaean fashion, as an evil—as if the whole process of manifestation were an unfortunate lapse from the infinite state to be escaped as soon as possible. From another, and more exact, point of view the Golden Age is the first state of manifestation prior to the development of ego-consciousness. It is the 'natural' state of primitivity and infancy wherein consciousness is so fascinated and so absorbed in externals that it does not reflect upon itself. It is probable, however, that this period is 'Golden' mostly from the standpoint of nostalgic retrospect. It is not without its full share of suffering, labour and struggle for existence. But all this suffering has a momentary character because of the absorption of consciousness in the present. The sense of ego comes to birth with the growth of memory and anticipation, resulting in the experience of an ego-unity 'transcending' the stream of events.

The small child can switch emotions with astonishing rapidity; at one moment it can be shedding tears, and at the next laughing as if nothing had happened. The past does not carry over into the present, and life is so full of novelty and surprise that there is neither time nor occasion for clinging to memories. While the analogy between the infant and primitive man may be pressed too far, there is the same absence of any real sense of history and time, the same lack of sophistication, the same capacity to abandon oneself without the least restraint or awkwardness to the present moment and its mood. For the ego represents man's bondage to past and future; at any given moment it hardly exists at all, but as soon as past and present experiences, and future anticipations, are linked into a chain the ego exists. Past sufferings and fears for the future then enter the present and fill it with new and impossible problems beyond immediate solution. Past joys are eagerly retained in memory, and upon them are based hopes for the future which become the chief impulse to present work, with the result that the immediate reality of the moment loses its fascination. The individual gathers experiences to himself instead of losing himself in them, and from these is fashioned the cocoon of the ego from which the self is eventually to break.

But because life is a flux which resists being woven into a fixed form, which constantly eludes our schemes to possess it, the task of maintaining the ego is full of heartbreaks and frustrations. Naturally, then, man looks back with a certain nostalgia to the time when he could fearlessly and irresponsibly let himself go to the passing mood. He fabricates dreams of an age when the flux of nature could be trusted, when he could live securely without resort to plans and artificiality, when nature fed him without the necessity of labour, and when the poison of death had not entered the world. Of course the natural situation was then as it is now; men worked and suffered and died, but because of the absence of any real experience of the ego, work, suffering, and death were not problematic. Work and suffering were of the moment. This moment's pain did not involve the thought of all past and future pains. The death of another was objective and external; it did not involve the thought of one's own inevitable extinction.

'In the Golden Age, good men were not appreciated; ability was not conspicuous. Rulers were mere beacons, while the people were as free as the wild deer. They were upright without being conscious of duty to their neighbours. They loved one another without being conscious of charity. They were true without being conscious of loyalty. They were honest without being conscious of good faith. They acted freely in all things without recognizing obligations to any one. Thus, their deeds left no trace; their affairs were not handed down to posterity.'[1]

Goodness, charity, loyalty and honesty are, along with the ego itself, *abstractions* from experience, and the power to abstract, differentiate and discriminate is a relatively late development in man. The primitive state is one of uniformity and undifferentiation for which Lévy-Brühl has coined the term *participation mystique*, having approximately the same sense as the psychological term 'projection', the identification of subject and object, the confusion of psychic with external experience.

'It must be remembered that our individual conscious psychology develops out of an original state of unconsciousness, or in other words, a non-differentiated condition. . . . Consciousness of distinctiveness, therefore, is a relatively late achievement of mankind—and presumably a relatively small section of the indefinitely large field of original identification. Discrimination is the essence, the *conditio sine qua non* of consciousness.'[2]

We refer to the child and the primitive as unconscious not, of course, because they have no awareness, but because the peculiarly ego-conscious powers of discrimination are undeveloped. The individual has not acquired enough psychic 'property' to become a 'man of distinction'.

This first stage represents, then, the maximum identification of the infinite with the finite, of the Self with the objects in its point of view. In retrospect it is a period of harmony and unity because we look back upon it from a period of conflict. From its own standpoint, however, the idea of harmony between man

[1] *Chuang-tzu*, xii. Trs. H. A. Giles.

[2] C. G. Jung, *Collected Works*, Vol. 7, *Two Essays in Analytical Psychology* (Princeton, N.J., 1953), par. 329.

and his universe would be meaningless since there has never been any important distinction between the two.[1]

Because, then, of the harmony, the timelessness, and the ego-lessness of the primitive state it is often used as an analogy for the state of supreme realization. 'Except ye be converted and become as little children, ye cannot enter into the kingdom of God'. Spiritual illumination is therefore described as 'second birth', as a *return* to the original Paradise or Eden, to the Great Father or Mother from whom we issued, a return initiated by an act of *repentance* or 'turning around'. This analogy has made it possible for certain psychologists to represent the religious or mystical life as a sort of infantilism, a resistance to growth, a desire to return to the womb and escape the stark loneliness and responsibility of ego-consciousness and manhood.

While it is no doubt true that man resists his separation from the mother and very often uses religion as a convenient projection of his desire to slide downhill, the strictly analogical nature of these comparisons cannot be too strongly stressed. Meta-physical realization lies only *through* the stage of ego-conscious-ness, with all its conflicts and struggles, with all the frightful burden of responsibility and guilt which pertains to it. For the sense of extreme isolation, of extreme opposition to God on the one hand and his universe on the other, is the one essential pre-paration for the consciousness of union. There is no road back save into neurosis and ever deeper frustration and guilt, as is well exemplified in modern man's attempted escape from the Christian sense of our eternal destiny and of our Godlike and catastrophic freedom.

It is for this reason, then, that the primitive state of identifica-tion with the mother, of psychic harmony through the confusion of subject and object, has to be brought to an end by the 'truly necessary sin of Adam'. Man has to become as a god, knowing good and evil. He has to eat of the tree of knowledge, whereby he becomes conscious of himself and his own naked-ness. Conscious of himself, his nakedness and his need of pro-tection, he becomes aware of the conflict between himself and nature—'cursed is the ground for thy sake'—and of the death that will certainly overwhelm him. The acquisition of this

[1] It is possible that this lack of distinction is reflected in the absence of perspective in primitive art, for perspective is a conven-tion to show the *distance* between percipient and objects.

knowledge automatically exiles him from the Garden of Eden, the state of primitive unconsciousness, and sends him out into the world *alone*.

In the terms of metaphysic, the Self is beginning to awaken. It has ceased to identify itself with the *totality* of experience. It is now identified only with the more proximate objects in the field of consciousness, with the body, with the inner psychic life of thought and feeling and desire, and with the system of memory and anticipation which secures the ego as an entity persisting amid the flux of events. At first undifferentiated and vague, the field of consciousness next includes distinct objects, and then becomes polarized into subject and object, I and Thou, self and other. But because the true centre is still unconscious of itself and is identified with things which, because they are finite objects, are essentially impermanent, the Self experiences anxiety and dread. To protect its vehicle, the ego, from dissolution there must be a struggle for security, for property, for power, for ecstasy, for virtue and respectability.

Naturally this anxiety issues in sin, because the Self mistakes its own true good for the immediate good of the ego. Sin, however, brings inevitable frustration simply because of the finite nature of all goods less than the infinite itself. Wealth, power, pleasure and security are mere substitutes for the eternal Father whom the Son innately desires; but because of his identification with the ego, the Son identifies his innate desire with the desires of the ego. But the certain frustration of those desires serves only to awaken the Self yet more, until it comes to the realization that its true end does not lie within the realm of finite objects at all.

It is at this point that the phase of involution ends. Still in the midst of ego-consciousness, man realizes that what he wants is God. But because he is now at that place on the cycle of life which lies directly opposite the place of origin, and because at this stage the sense of ego, through repeated frustration, is at its most lonely, most desolate and most guilty nadir of experience, God seems unutterably other and remote. At this stage it is absolutely inconceivable that the Self and the infinite are one; assimilated entirely to the solitary ego, the Self calls to its consubstantial Father out of the deep for grace and forgiveness. 'I will arise and go to my Father and say unto him, "Father I have sinned against heaven and in thy sight, and am no more worthy to be called thy son; make me as one of thy hired servants".'

The call from the deep is answered. Because the Self and ego, spirit and soul, are still identified, the answer comes in an indirect and analogical form. An event transpiring in the yet unconscious centre of man's being is projected upon an external symbol. God the Father sends down a historic or mythological Saviour both divine and human, in Christianity the Christ, and in oriental traditions the Avatar of Vishnu, the Buddha or the individual *guru* or spiritual director. For excellent reasons it cannot at this stage become known that the primary locus of this event is within the Self, that, as Jung would say, the external Saviour or Teacher is a figure who receives the projection of an internal and unconscious 'archetype'.

Before the Self can realize its true nature, the most intense phase of the struggle has yet to come. It cannot know its distinction from the ego until, as the ego, it has tried to master the ego and conform it to the likeness of God as expressed in the divine-human figure of the Saviour. Thus the Saviour is known externally as a companion and helper in the struggle, and only the most fragmentary hints ever reach consciousness of the fact that he is the One within us who struggles. No longer, then, is the conflict between the ego and external events, but between the ego and itself. With the external Saviour as exemplar and comforter and source of power, the ego tries to drag itself up to the stature of divinity by asceticism, penance and prayer—all the while becoming more and more conscious of its own vanity, sinfulness and impotence.

Wrestling with itself, confessing its sins, examining its conscience, attempting to curb its appetites and to crush its pride, the ego is increasingly 'saved' from the darkness of unconsciousness. It learns to know itself through and through. But the more it knows itself, the more vividly the conviction grows that it cannot change itself, that it cannot eradicate its pride, that it cannot conform itself to the image of God. Strangling pride, it grows proud of its humility. Getting rid of selfishness, it finds that it has done it for a selfish motive. The last word of religion on this predicament is 'God be merciful to me a sinner!' The final hope is to put implicit trust in the power and the promises of the external Saviour. These are, from the religious standpoint, the final aspirations of the dying person who has to give up the struggle long before its completion.

Religion as such carries us beyond this point only in dark sayings and hidden meanings. From the mystical and meta-physical points of view the struggle reaches its climax and *impasse* in the midst of life rather than at the moment of physical death. Going beyond this climax, the mystic becomes aware of things which, if expressed in religious terms, invariably make him suspect of heresy.

> 'I know that without me
> God can no moment live;
> Were I to die, then He
> No longer could survive.
>
> I am as great as God,
> And He is small like me;
> He cannot be above,
> Nor I below Him be.'[1]

For at the moment when the ego surrenders and gives up the battle, finding that the attempt to make itself like God is bound to fail, the Self awakens to its own independence. In surrender the ego thoroughly accepts and admits its own finitude. But who accepts? Who *knows* the finitude of the ego? In reality, the Self has at last given up its identification with the ego, perceiving the ego as a finite object quite distinct from its own proper being. And in that instant the Self knows its own eternity and infinity, realizing that from the beginning the entire drama has had no more effect upon its essential nature than the ripples in a pool upon the sun whose reflected image they break and scatter.

Fundamentally, then, the coming of realization depends upon the will of the Self, which in religion is called the divine grace. By its own will it identifies itself with the finite world; by its own will it realizes its essential freedom and eternity, as one who in the midst of a dream knows he is dreaming. But in this connection the dream is not something to be forgotten and left behind in the past, for that which the Self has loved, to which it has so faithfully abandoned its consciousness, in which it has

[1] *Angelus Silesius.*

willed to be so wholly absorbed, is no mere phantasm; it is its own finite image, the splendid representation of the *logos* in terms of time, space and form.

For this reason the finite point of view is not left behind; the Self does not immediately 'quit' the ego, the soul-body, and revert to primal omniscience. On the contrary, it wills its own will consciously and continues quite deliberately to give itself to the limitations of finite life. In this it is profoundly true to its own nature, for, as we have seen, it is not the nature of the infinite to be 'stand-offish', to separate itself from its own creation. It remains, therefore, 'in most loving bondage, free'.

This perfect consistency of realized identity with the infinite Self and continuance in the finite world is perhaps one of the most important and least understood aspects of metaphysical doctrine. There will be occasion to deal with it at some length in the next chapter. But two observations are called for at this point. The first is that this state is the supreme realization of non-duality, of the absolute compatibility of the infinite and finite viewpoints, of the truth that finite and physical existence presents no obstacle whatsoever to the infinite. To put it in another way, the infinite does not lose its omniscience while simultaneously assuming a finite point of view.

The second observation follows from the first. It is obvious that those who enjoy realization neither claim nor manifest omniscience, much less omnipotence, as egos. The reason is simply that there is no manifestation of omnipotence apart from the total finite order itself. In a certain sense, this universe *is* the manifestation of their omnipotence. Furthermore, in so far as we speak of *those* who realize, we are actually referring to their egos, to certain identifiable individuals in whom the Self is awakened. Omnipotence is, in the nature of things, not manifested through *an* individual but through all individuals. Again, in so far as the Self is awakened *in* those individuals, it retains the finite point of view. If it did not retain it, if the Self were to reassume omniscience, it could not in any case communicate that omniscience to the ego, to the finite faculties of reason, feeling and sense, and through them express it to others. In the face of omniscience, the faculties of the finite mind would find themselves utterly baffled and would thus be temporarily suspended. While they are no obstacle to omniscience, omniscience is an obstacle to them; obviously they cannot comprehend it at all.[1]

It is for this reason that metaphysical realization is no substitute for what Northrop terms the *theoretic* mode of knowledge proper to science. Realization does not communicate to the finite reason any knowledge of *how* the finite universe is produced, of what, for example, are the inner mysteries of nuclear physics. Such knowledge must still be acquired theoretically, that is to say, by reasoned reflection upon the results of certain experiments. The oriental traditions give no account of such knowledge not because metaphysic excludes it, but because their external development has lain along quite different lines. In principle, the theoretic knowledge of science may be pursued against the background of metaphysic quite as well as any other kind of knowledge.

The third stage of Self-consciousness, which concludes the phase of evolution, is thus a realization of the infinite within the limitations of finite life. The Vedanta describes persons in this stage as *jivan-mukti*, that is to say, liberated while the *atma* is still

[1] It is possible that the self awakens to its own omniscience in the state of *samadhi* where there is a complete suspension of the finite faculties. On emerging from *samadhi* there remains the intuition of a state of consciousness utterly surpassing description. Western mystics have sometimes tried to give accounts of it, but can only speak in terms at once confused and seemingly extravagant. 'In an instant . . . the mind learns so many things, that if the imagination and intellect spent many years in striving to enumerate them, it would be impossible to recall a thousandth part of them.' St. Teresa, *Interior Castle*, Sixth Mansion, v. 8. 'God is sometimes pleased, while a person is engaged in prayer, and in perfect possession of her senses, to suspend them and to discover sublime mysteries to her, which she appears to behold within God himself. . . . This is no imaginary vision, but a highly intellectual one, wherein is manifested how all things are beheld in God, and how he contains them within himself.' Ibid., x. 2. 'As he stood there praying, he was suddenly raised above himself in such a wonderful manner that he could not afterwards account for it, and the Lord revealed to him the whole beauty and glory of the firmament and of every created thing, so that his longing was fully satisfied. But afterwards, when he came to himself, the Prior could get nothing more out of him than that he had received such unspeakable rapture from his perfect knowledge of the creation, that it was beyond human understanding.' From the Life of Blessed Hermann Joseph, quoted by Poulain, *Graces of Interior Prayer* (London, 1910), p. 278.

associated with the *jiva* or ego. We can speak of what lies 'beyond' the third stage only analogically, because the conclusion of this stage brings consciousness to the end of time and succession. At this point consciousness 'ascends' to the eternal state, wherein the entire cycle is not obliterated but known simultaneously with its dark and light aspects, involution and evolution, seen in perfect harmony.

The question arises as to what becomes of those individuals who do not, in their lifetime, pass beyond the unconscious or ego-conscious stages. It is a total misunderstanding of the oriental doctrine to imagine that they contemplate a reincarnation of the ego-soul, or of the 'particular' Self (more accurately, the *buddhi*) associated with it, in another physical body. This is a purely exoteric and popular misinterpretation of a doctrine of post-mortem development having something in common with the religious concepts of Purgatory or the Intermediate State. The popular notion of reincarnation has no relevance at all, not the least reason being that from the eternal standpoint *every* life, every individual, in whatever stage he may have lived and died, has manifested an essential and integral part of the total finite harmony. Every point on the circle is equally close to the centre. Tragic as it may seem from the level of time and succession to die when no further than the darkest and most trying phases of ego-consciousness, the life so lived has not been in vain. For in eternity those phases are no absolute evil; they are as much of the essence of the total harmony as the burial of the seed is of the essence of the total growth of a plant. And, as we have seen, the apparent tragedy involves no harshness or unfairness of fate upon the invididuals concerned, because in every one of them the ultimate Experiencer of such tragedy is the Self. Certainly the individual ego, the soul-body, that lives and dies in the involutionary phase of the cycle is in a special sense 'judged' eternally. From the eternal standpoint that particular life is 'always' in the dark aspect of things, and in that very special sense subject to 'eternal damnation'. The evil perpetrated in that life is something done finally, both in time and eternity, and the specific actions concerned are never blotted out. But the essential Self involved in them is the real judge, and because his justice is identical with mercy and his wrath with love, the *only* eternal view of such 'damned' lives is one which knows them as integral threads in a fabric where dark and light are harmonized in perfect beauty.[1]

Having considered the cycle of involution and evolution from the standpoint of principle, we can now go on to see something of the way in which it is projected into religious and mythological symbolism. As already pointed out, the entire cycle may be regarded as the finite image and incarnation of the *logos*, God the Son, expressing his distinction from the Father in involution and his union with the Father in evolution. The entry of God the Son into the cycle may be seen as the Eternal Sacrifice, the voluntary abandonment of himself to the finite order, which he performs as the great High Priest—a sacrifice which is atoning because it is precisely what unites or 'at-ones' the finite and the infinite.

The religious doctrine very naturally confines the Incarnation and the Atonement to the second, evolutionary, phase of the cycle, for the reason that in the first phase the Son, having deliberately forgotten and abandoned his true identity, is 'in the dark', in the unconscious. But conscious atonement, conscious union, requires a preliminary separation. It is thus that the Son is recognized, that is, realized, in Christ but not in Adam, for in Adam the Word is hidden rather than made manifest in the flesh. From the religious point of view the 'dark' incarnation of the *logos* in Adam must remain a mystery, untaught because unknown as well as incomprehensible from the standpoint of ego-consciousness. The sacred texts can only present this dark incarnation in a veiled manner, by setting Christ as the Second Adam side by side with the First Adam in a highly suggestive parallelism.[2]

---

[1] Cf. Psalm 139: 'If I say, peradventure the darkness will cover me; then shall my night be turned into day. For the darkness is no darkness with Thee: the darkness and the light to Thee are both alike.' On the post-mortem development of the unawakened see Guénon's *Man and His Becoming According to the Vedanta* (London, 1945), pp. 120-161.

[2] Cf. the following texts: 'And God said, "Let us make man in our own image, after our likeness".' Genesis i. 26. 'God . . . hath in these last days spoken unto us by his Son, whom he hath appointed heir of all things, by whom also he made the worlds; who being the bright-

To understand this parallelism one must remember that true symbolism, as distinct from allegory, is not consciously constructed; it is the best intelligible representation of interior and unconscious contents, or inspirations of the Holy Ghost, which at the time of the symbol's production *cannot* be grasped in any better way.

'An expression that stands for a known thing always remains merely a sign and is never a symbol. It is therefore quite impossible to make a living symbol, i.e. one that is pregnant with meaning, from known associations. . . . Every psychic product, in so far as it is the best possible expression at the moment for a fact as yet unknown or only relatively known, may be regarded as a symbol, provided also that we are prepared to accept the expression as designating something that is only divined and not yet clearly conscious.'[1]

Just because the symbol is not a conscious and rational artifice, it represents its underlying meaning in a naïve manner, by simple association rather than logical connection. Therefore it is impossible to show an exact and mechanical correspondence of symbols to metaphysical principles, or of various systems of symbols to each other. Symbolism is invariably suggestive rather than indicative.

If this is borne in mind the connection between Adam and Christ, as between the First Creation and the New Creation, is one of profound correspondence. As the First Creation proceeds from the Spirit of God moving upon the face of the waters, the New Creation of the 'new man' in Baptism is 'by water and the Spirit'. Likewise the Christ is conceived by the Holy Spirit and born of the Virgin Mary, whom the liturgy of Holy Saturday associates with the 'immaculate womb' of the baptismal font. As Adam is created by the conjunction of the breath or spirit of God and the dust of the earth, so Christ emerges from the Spirit and the *Mater Virgo*, or 'virgin matter', both earth and

---

ness of his glory, and the *express image* of his person.' Hebrews i. 1-3. 'And the Lord God formed man of the dust of the ground, and breathed into his nostrils the breath of life.' Genesis ii. 7. 'Then shall the dust return to the earth as it was: and the spirit shall return unto God who gave it.' Ecclesiastes xii. 7. 'The first man Adam became a living soul. The last Adam became a life-giving spirit.' 1 Corinthians xv. 45. Cf. also Luke iii. 23-38, esp. 38.

[1] Jung, *Collected Works*, Vol. 6, *Psychological Types*, par. 817.

water being traditionally feminine symbols as against the masculine symbols of air and fire which denote the spirit.[1]

More arresting than the parallel between the birth of Adam, the First Image, and Christ, the Second Image of God, is the parallel of Fall and Crucifixion so clearly noted in the liturgical Preface of the Cross:

'Who didst set the salvation of mankind upon the tree of the cross, so that whence came death, thence also life might rise again, and he (Satan) who by the tree was vanquisher might also by the tree be vanquished.'

St. John's Gospel employs the serpent of bronze (*nehushtan*) raised by Moses in the wilderness for the healing of a plague as a type for the lifting up of the Son of Man on the cross, and there is the most obvious parallel between the serpent of healing and the serpent of poison on the Tree of Knowledge.[2] The two serpents of poison and healing appear on the tree of the Caduceus, symbol of medicine and of the healing principle *similia similibus curantur* (like cures like), and in some parts of the Eastern Church the Caduceus has become the pastoral staff of bishops. Two serpents, one pointing down and the other up, constitute the movements of involution and evolution respectively, and appear again as fish in the Zodiacal sign of Pisces so commonly found on early Christian engraved gems and other objects of liturgical art.[3]

Despite the conscious opposition of the early Church to astrology, a considerable amount of astrological symbolism has entered Christian iconography. The bull, lion, eagle (an alternate symbol for the scorpion and phoenix), and man used as signs for the four Evangelists are the four fixed signs of the

[1] We have not space here to enter into the extremely complex and fascinating web of associations between *mater* and *materia*, between the idea of the mother and the earth, or between Mary (Miriam) and water, or again between Mary as the mother of Christ (the New Law) and Miriam as foster-mother of Moses (the Old Law), watching over his crib on the waters of the Nile, or celebrating the emergence of the Israelites from the Red Sea. Typological affinity between the Old and New Testaments had a profound fascination for the actual writers of the New Testament as well as for Christians as a whole until the close of the Middle Ages.

[2] John iii. 14.

[3] For examples see Lowrie, *Art in the Early Church* (New York, 1947), pl. 32. Also British Museum, *Guide to Early Christian and Byzantine Antiquities* (London, 1903), p. 17.

Zodiac—Taurus, Leo, Scorpio and Aquarius. Pisces, however, is the Christian sign *par excellence*, both because it is the *end* of the signs of the Zodiac and thus of the domination of the spirit by the stars, and also because the coming of the Christian era coincides approximately with the entry of the sun into Pisces in the equinoctial procession. Cosmological correspondences of this kind are indeed arbitrary and fatuous to the modern mind. But symbolism is a system of association revealing not logic but the inner and unknown spiritual life of man.[1]

Christian imagination connects not only the two opposed serpents or fishes but also the two trees, the Tree of Knowledge and the Tree of the Cross. Obscure in origin, there is a whole corpus of legend concerning the wood of the cross as grown from a cutting taken by Seth from the Tree of Knowledge.[2] Once again, however fanciful and late in development this or any other item of Christian symbolism may be, the study of the meaning of Christianity cannot be confined to the study of its historical origins just as the oak is not to be understood from the acorn. It is as much a principle of symbology as of theology that Christianity is a living organism, which, as it grows in time, develops things that were potential in the seed. To imagine that the development of doctrine and symbolism is a mere acquisition of unessential accretions is like thinking that the complex structure of man is a mere collection of odds and ends obscuring the pure and original protoplasm.

Serpent and tree stand opposite fish and cross as the beginning and the end of the ego-conscious stage. In Adam the *logos* is incarnate unconsciously, and in Adam he falls with the downward serpent of involution into the isolation of ego-consciousness, so expressing the extreme limit of his distinction from the Father.

[1] With an almost uncanny appropriateness the sign of Pisces is polarized with the sign of Virgo. Pisces represents both fulfilment and dissolution, and thus as the Christian sign it marks the dissolution of the spirit's subjection to elemental forces, the end of the world where 'world' is understood as belonging to the unholy trinity of the world, the flesh and the devil. It should be noted that astrological symbolism has no necessary connection with the objective stars, but is more probably a projection upon the external universe of the Zodiac considered as a basic symbol of the rhythm of life.

[2] de Voragine, *The Golden Legend*. Trs. Ryan and Ripperger (New York, 1941), p. 269 f. Rappoport, *Mediaeval Legends of Christ* (New York, 1935), pp. 210-234.

At the very nadir of the cycle the involutionary movement ends, and turning or repenting in his course the *logos* begins again to be conscious of his relation to the Father. Still identified with the ego, the Self realizes that in some way it belongs to God. This birth of the consciousness of sonship, a consciousness yet in its infancy, begins the movement of evolution. It is Christmas, the birth of the child Christ, which occurs appropriately enough at the Winter Solstice, the nadir of the year when the

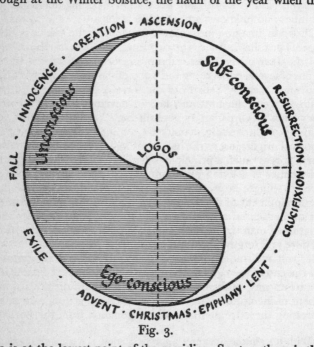

CREATION · ASCENSION
INNOCENCE
Unconscious
Self-conscious
FALL
RESURRECTION
LOGOS
CRUCIFIXION
EXILE
Ego-conscious
ADVENT · CHRISTMAS · EPIPHANY · LENT

Fig. 3.

sun is at the lowest point of the meridian. So, too, there is the tradition that Christ was born not only at the Winter Solstice but also at midnight, both being places from which the sun begins its return.

The child Christ grows to manhood, and likewise by effort and discipline the ego matures its longing for God under the spur of the wakening Self. Finally, the Self has to surrender the ego as on the cross the Son of God surrenders his humanity. As the resurrection follows the crucifixion, realization follows the

158

surrender of the ego, and as the body of Christ rises glorified from the dead, finite life is not ended with realization but brought to its proper perfection as the instrument and conscious expression of the Self. The whole cycle culminates in the Ascension. Just as Christ ascends *with his body* into heaven, so the Self at last ascends to the eternal point of view where the 'body' of finite existence is not left behind but seen in its total harmony and glory—the image of the *logos*, separate from and yet one with the Father.

Obviously the evolutionary phase of the cycle harmonizes perfectly with the seasons of the Church calendar—beginning with the repentance of Advent, followed by Christmas, the dawning light of Epiphany, the discipline of Lent, the desolation of the Passion, the sudden awakening of Easter, the Forty Days of the Risen Christ on earth corresponding to the entire third or Self-conscious stage, which culminates at last in the supreme triumph of the Ascension. The coincidence of Easter with the moment of realization in the metaphysical order is further emphasized by the fact that Easter Eve is the traditional occasion for Baptism, for initiation into the Body of Christ.

As is well known, the catechumens or candidates for Baptism were prepared and instructed for perhaps as much as a year beforehand, the preparation reaching its height in Lent and Holy Week. Assembling in the basilica on Holy Saturday, vigil was kept until dark, when, after the benediction of fire and the Paschal Candle, the litanies and prophecies were chanted, and the font blessed. Following Baptism, the Mass was celebrated after midnight when the newly initiated received Communion with all the faithful. The rite of Holy Saturday in the missal, comprising the blessing of fire and the candle, as well as the font, contains some of the most profoundly mystical passages in the entire liturgy of the Church. It has, indeed, the character of a sort of initiatory discourse, touching on the deepest mysteries of religion, and is especially concerned with the emergence of light from the midst of darkness, and the mysterious necessity of the darkness to the coming of the light.

It is not suggested that the ancient Church possessed, as a corporate body, any 'secret knowledge' not handed down to later times which was revealed on these occasions. What is truly esoteric is 'secret' for the sole and simple reason that language cannot express it, or that anything esoteric which can be expressed in some degree is merely unintelligible to those unprepared to receive it. The point is simply that, with or without conscious intent on the part of individual Christians, Christian doctrine, symbolism and liturgy constitute a very perfect and beautiful analogy of the eternal principles.

It is of interest that the Church year has a definite form during only half of the Solar year. The long period of Sundays after Pentecost (or Trinity) is without any organized character, and it is possible that this formlessness of half the year has some connection with the fact that the religious point of view must be unconscious of the dark or hidden incarnation of the Son in Adam.

Once it is expressed in religious terms, the idea of the 'dark' incarnation must of course seem both strange and dangerous to the religious mind. But we are far from suggesting that anything of this kind be incorporated in the formal and dogmatic teaching of religion. On the contrary, in so far as the religious point of view is peculiarly adapted to the ego-conscious stage of man's life, it is almost necessary that the dark incarnation remain dark. So long as the Self is identified with the ego, the Supreme Identity may be vaguely intelligible as theory but is so strange and foreign to one's basic intuition and attitude to life that it is really incomprehensible.

Of necessity the religious mind is suspicious of metaphysical 'claims', because it seems to suggest the existence of an exclusive circle of esoteric 'elect' beyond the normal life and discipline of the Church. Self-styled *illuminati* have existed often enough within the Church, and have been notable chiefly for their overweening spiritual pride. Probably the most glaring sign of such pride is the very claim to be free from it. But the essence of metaphysical realization is that the whole idea of *claiming* anything is utterly foreign to it. One simply cannot say, '*I* have realized the Supreme Identity' without uttering a complete contradiction, for, as we have said before, it is the Self and not the ego which realizes, and the Self is no one's property. It must be repeated again that so long as the ego exists at all, it must worship. Reason, feeling and sense must ever relate themselves to the Self as to God, venerating him as other and infinitely superior. Incarnate God as he was, Jesus worshipped alone and in the temple, and not merely to set a good example to his disciples. Even the supposedly 'godless' Buddhists have their worship, a worship by no means confined to the exoteric and uninitiated masses.[1] The person who feels that the Supreme Identity excludes worship as unnecessary and illogical is a mere monist, for non-duality, the infinite, the Self, is what it is just because it can accept and include duality.

On the other hand, pride also cloaks itself under false modesty, and is furthermore quite rampant in the mob which refuses to recognize that an elect really does exist. The Church admits to a moral elect in the saints, although saints confess themselves sinners. It is possible to admit also to an intellectual elect, although such persons invariably confess themselves fools, asserting that as egos they do not know the ultimate Reality at all.

'If you think that you know *Brahma* well, what you know of Its nature is in reality but little; for this reason *Brahma* should be still more attentively considered by you. . . . Whoever among us understands the following words: "I do not know It, and yet I know It," verily that man knows it. He who thinks that *Brahma* is not comprehended, by him *Brahma* is comprehended; but he who thinks that *Brahma* is comprehended knows It not. *Brahma* is unknown to those who know It and is known to those who do not know It at all.'[2]

In other words, the *gnosis* of metaphysical realization is not the proud *gnosis* which in its early centuries the Church very properly rejected. Ever since, the Latin Church in particular has remained unfriendly to gnosticism of any kind, the official Thomist position being that all human knowledge whatsoever is analogical sense knowledge. One cannot object to this position if the definition of the human being is restricted to the ego, but as Thomism confuses the ego and the Self, the soul and the spirit, it amounts in practice to a rejection of the *gnosis*. This gives a certain truth to Berdyaev's observation that, 'official theology has preferred scientific positivism and a mechanistic theory of nature to any form of cosmological gnosis. Better a godless world than one regarded as divine. . . . The

[1] Several very deeply enlightened orientals have impressed the author as some of the most reverent people he has known.

[2] *Kena Upanishad*, ii. 1-3. Trs. Guénon-Nicholson. Cf. St. Diony sius, *Ep. ad Gaium Therapeutem:* 'And if anyone, seeing God, were to understand what he saw, he would not have seen God, but some one of his creatures that exist and may be known.'

mind of the Church in our day is losing more and more its cosmic nature. The Church is beginning to be regarded as a community of believers, as an institution; dogmas are being interpreted from the moralistic standpoint, and the psychological aspect of the sacraments is stressed at the expense of their cosmic significance.'[1]

In other words, where the *gnosis* is absent the Church loses the realization that it constitutes an analogy of universal principles. Cosmology is the recognition that the universe as a cosmos, an order of involution and evolution, is the finite expression of the *logos*, of the creative will of the infinite, and that therefore its basic order corresponds analogically with the order of religion.

Because of its absorption in historicism and moralism religion finds itself concurring with modern science and philosophy in the rejection of metaphysical knowledge and certainty. Under such circumstances, all attempts to rectify the social order, to 'apply' religion to the political and economic problems of the world, will, in the long run, be nothing more than a dissipation of energy. Not only is the social order incomprehensible apart from the cosmological order, but without metaphysical knowledge religion is a wheel spinning by momentum alone, and now running dangerously slow. To perform the desired work of bringing sanity into the world, religion must order itself not only to what is below it but also to what is above it. The wheel must be connected to the source of power.

But Christian experience feels the source of power to lie in charity rather than knowledge, and is suspicious of metaphysic for the very reason that it seems to exalt knowing above loving. Yet it is impossible to separate metaphysical knowledge from divine charity; in realization knowledge and love are one, and the identity of the two is found in the ancient use of the verb 'to know' in speaking of the love between man and woman. The knowledge of the Self is not that so-called knowledge which gives spiritual pride, a knowledge which should more correctly be called information. To know the ultimate Reality is to know and be one with *caritas* itself.

Christianity has found the supreme expression of the divine charity in the crucified Christ, because the love of God whereby 'the sun and other stars' are moved is nothing other than sacrifice. For sacrifice voluntarily made is that very self-abandon-

[1] *Freedom and the Spirit* (London, 1935), p. 289.

ment of the infinite to the finite which causes the universe to exist. The cross moves the world. The seemingly grim fact that life feeds on life, that we exist by devouring other creatures, is only explained finally in the cross and the eucharist. Life is maintained by a mutual sacrifice; in all eating and drinking the Body is broken and the Blood is shed for us, because the whole creation expresses that Logos who is 'the Lamb slain from the foundation of the world'.

To realize union with the infinite is to be one with that which gives itself limitlessly. Metaphysical knowledge demands that we take the greatest risks and surrender our craving for individual certainty and security. The reason why some find it hard to perceive charity in the metaphysical order is that we are here beyond the range of sentiment. It is natural enough that the love of God be confused with sentimental love, with emotions, but any good theologian knows that charity is a motion of the will rather than the feelings. From the sentimental point of view, which is rightly and necessarily operative in religion, metaphysic must always seem cold. But without that intellectual charity which is of will rather than emotion, sentimental love is a mere effervescence which shortly gives out.

But despite the theological recognition that charity is of the will, in practice the religious mind has it hopelessly confused with sentiment, and for that reason cannot understand it in terms of the Supreme Identity. Religion believes that here there can be no love without an eternal and absolute dualism of subject and object, because sentimental love *needs* an object. Sentimental love expresses *eros* rather than *agape*, the love of hunger rather than of generosity, because of the insufficiency of the finite. But the charity of the infinite is no hunger because there is no insufficiency. It does not need an object. By abandonment of itself, without the least necessity to do so, it *creates* an object.

# V. THE WAY OF REALIZATION

## OUTLINE

All the foregoing theory and doctrine is unsatisfactory apart from effective realization—upon which it is based. How is this attained?

1. To ask, 'How can *I* attain realization?' is the wrong question if by 'I' is meant the ego, for the Self, not the ego, realizes. If by 'I' is meant the Self, the question is absurd, because the Self does not *need* to realize on account of its inherent and essential infinity. Realization comes only when the Self wills it freely, without necessity. Can we then do nothing?

2. The Self will not let us do nothing. As soon as we begin to desire realization, this is the sign that the process has begun. Our search for the Self is moved by the Self. To become, or realize, what we are, we must first *try* to become it, in order to realize effectively that it is not necessary to do so. The various methods of trying:

   i. Prayer and meditation upon God.
   ii. Concentration or *yoga*-practice.
   iii. Detachment—or *letting go* the contents of consciousness.
   iv. Living in the eternal Now.

3. The state of realization compared with the religious aim of contemplating God as an *object* of knowledge. The difficulty created by the fact that the contemplation of God as an object annihilates all other objects, creating the tension in religion between theocentric mysticism and active charity.

God, as the Self, is known interiorly, as the inmost Subject, for the subjective realm is not opposed to the objective, whereas objects are mutually exclusive. Hence the perfect compatibility of realization with everyday experience.

Realization of the Supreme Identity is found, not through seeking it as remote and obscure, but in accepting the truth that nothing is more obvious and self-evident.

# V. THE WAY OF REALIZATION

As simple theory, all that has been said thus far is obviously unsatisfactory. Ideas are one thing; knowledge is quite another, and this is the more so when the ideas composing the theory are not positive ideas at all but negative concepts, hinting at what lies beyond time and space by describing their limitations. In comparison with the colourful and moving terms of religion, the language of metaphysical doctrine is abstract and cold. In comparison with the clear logic and reasonable coherence of a great theology, the form of metaphysical thought is confused with paradox and hardly intelligible to reason at all. In trying to grasp such doctrine the mind reels dizzily as if it were standing on the brink of ultimate Nothing. It will be no occasion for surprise if, fearing for its own sanity, the mind retreats to the comfortable realm of relativity and tries its best to believe in finite and determinate absolutes, ignoring the contradictions involved.

Yet the theory of metaphysic as it has been presented is no mere straining of the reason at its own limits. It is a necessarily inadequate attempt to describe a most definite and positive experience which, hard as it may be to believe, is at once the most creative and the most satisfying experience possible. This, and not idle speculation, is the ground and origin of the doctrine. From the standpoint of actual realization the concept of non-duality is no web of paradox but simplicity itself, and the mystery of Supreme Identity is no fanciful opinion but clear certainty. Yet for all its simplicity and certainty, the sheer wonder of metaphysical knowledge is never exhausted. Therefore the great question whose importance surpasses all others is, 'How does one realize?'

[i]

Before we can consider any of the ways of realization which tradition has handed down to us, we must examine the question itself. To ask, 'How can I attain metaphysical knowledge, how can I know the infinite Reality?' is perhaps to ask the wrong question. For if the 'I' in the question is the ego, the answer is that you cannot attain realization. The apprehension of the infinite is altogether beyond the powers of reason, feeling and sense, save by analogy, and the attempt to make such knowledge a possession of the soul is not only doomed to failure but shows a total misunderstanding of its nature. The desire of the ego to attain realization or to make God its own property implies that very confusion of the Self with the ego which realization dissolves.

This explains the highly problematic character of spiritual exercises and techniques as they are generally practised. To try to make God an object of knowledge, to try to seek him, or to set out upon some course of spiritual development whose object is a *future* enjoyment of God, is, from one point of view, only to set God at a distance. Indeed, the remoteness, the absolute otherness of God is the presupposition of the ego-conscious point of view. Therefore all these attempts merely confirm the ego in its feeling of the remoteness of God, because they are precisely manifestations of that feeling. To look for God as an object implies his distance from the knowing subject. To seek for him implies his absence. To set him in the future is to imply that he is not eternal and present.

The same thing can be said in several other ways. The *Cloud of Unknowing* says that 'by love he may be gotten and holden'. Yet how can the ego love God? If love is the total surrender of oneself to God, how can I truly surrender myself if my basic reason for desiring to do so is that *I* want to get God? If the *sine qua non* of the knowledge of God is self-denial, one has only to ask why the ego wants to deny itself to find a selfish motive at the very root of the proposed denial. The ego humbles itself in order to be exalted, and by that very motive annihilates its humility. This is simply the ancient problem of grace stated in a slightly different way. Obviously one must have God's grace in order to love God, and we are told that this grace is freely offered to all; it has only to be accepted. But why do I want to accept it? The answer is inevitably that I want it because of self-love, that I accept it for a motive that denies it.

No one can read the writings of Krishnamurti, for example, and escape the relentless logic with which he reduces the longing for eternal life to the very cause which prevents our awareness of it—the desire for security. Feeling insecure, the ego desires God, eternal life, religion or mystical experience in order to escape from the suffering and loneliness of its position. In other words, the ego tries to escape from the all-consuming flux of life by attempting to possess it in certain fixed forms—the unchanging God, the infallible authority of the Church, or the immortal life of heaven. But the moment life is fixed, it is dead. In trying to make life a permanent possession of the ego, we are, as it were, destroying it by strangulation. The life so grasped by the ego is no more living than water caught up from the stream is flowing. Thus our spiritual methods, our moral laws, our religious authorities, are all so many escapes from insecurity whereby we destroy the thing we love. We must learn, then, says Krishnamurti, to be vividly aware of insecurity and suffering, of each moment of experience, instead of trying to run away from it, instead of trying to force it to conform to any fixed pattern or standard. Through such awareness, such total and unreserved acceptance of present reality, the true eternal life is known. 'He that would save his life shall lose it.' But the desire for God is the desire to be saved.

For these reasons the practice of a religion, the life of the Church as one sees it from day to day, often gives the impression of a multitude walking in the wrong direction on the right street. The discipline whose proper end is realization or union with God is adopted for an egoistic motive, and therefore seems only to confirm the soul in its egoism. The outward form of life changes, but the inner disposition remains. The wolf adopts sheep's clothing, even to the point of deceiving himself as well as others. The more perceptive, however, are not deceived. They know they are wolves. The greater the saint, the more certainly he knows that he is a miserable sinner, that the core of pride and self-love in the heart of the ego is simply ineradicable. Yet he keeps on in the faith that though with men it is not possible, with God all things are possible. But, as will be seen, the fact that he knows his own ego so thoroughly and is not deceived by it at all indicates the beginning of a shift of centre from the ego to the Self.

In short, then, there is no action whereby the ego can, of itself, produce or attain realization. As Shankara insists again and again, realization is the fruit of knowledge not action; it is the dissolution of nescience (*avidya*) or unconsciousness, and as darkness is not thrust aside by waving one's arms but only by the appearance of light, so nescience is overcome by knowing and not doing. Thus he argues that if action could produce realization, a realization so attained would not be eternal.

'Release (or realization, *moksha*) is shown to be of the nature of the eternally free Self, (and) it cannot be charged with the imperfection of non-eternality. Those, on the other hand, who consider Release to be something to be *effected*, properly maintain that it depends on the action of mind, speech, or body. . . . Non-eternality of Release is the certain consequence of these . . . opinions; for we observe in common life that . . . things which are effects, such as jars, etc., are non-eternal. Nor, again, can it be said that there is a dependence on action in consequence of (Release) being something which is to be obtained; for as Brahman constitutes a person's Self it is not something to be attained by that person. And even if Brahman were altogether different from a person's Self, still it would not be something to be obtained; for as it is omnipresent it is part of its nature that it is ever present to everyone.'[1]

Perhaps, then, the form of the preliminary question should be changed. Instead of asking how I, as ego, can attain realization, it may be that one should ask how I as the Self can attain it, by what method the Self in me can realize its true nature. This question, however, is irrelevant because the Self no more *needs* to realize itself than a light needs to illumine itself; as Shankara says, realization 'is shown to be of the nature of the eternally free Self'. This apparent paradox can be clarified when we see that the question involves three absurdities.

The first is that the question implies making the Self the *object* of its own knowledge, and as has been said before the Self knows itself immediately and subjectively, not mediately and objectively.

'Thou couldst not see the seer of sight, thou couldst not hear the hearer of hearing, nor perceive the perceiver of perception, nor know the knower of knowledge.'[2]

The same idea is expressed in one of the principal texts of Zen Buddhism, written by Hsi-yun:

'By their very seeking for it they produce the contrary effect

[1] Commentary on *Vedanta Sutras*, I. i. 4. Trs. G. Thibaut, in *SBE*, vol. xxxiv, pp. 32-33.
[2] *Brihadaranyaka Upanishad*, iii. 4. 2. Trs. G. Thibaut.

of losing it, for that is using the Buddha to seek for the Buddha and using mind (the Self) to grasp mind. . . . If it is held that there is something to be realized or attained apart from mind and, thereupon, mind is used to seek it, (that implies) failure to understand that mind and the object of its search are one. Mind cannot be used to seek something from mind for, even after the passage of millions of kalpas (aeons), the day of success would never come.'[1]

The second absurdity follows immediately from the first, namely that the notion of the Self seeking the Self implies and perpetuates that very confusion of the Self with the ego whereby realization is obscured. Once again, then, the very search for God or the Self as an object of knowledge presupposes the separation of God from the knowing and seeking subject—a presupposition which defeats the purpose of the search.

The third is the supposition that the Self *needs* to do or to be something other than what it is now willing or being. We have seen that the identification of Self and ego is a state which the Self voluntarily and freely wills, so that one is in the stage of ego-consciousness because that is where the Self wills to be. It must, however, be remembered that here, and in all that we are about to say, the act of *willing* is attributed to the Self analogically. There are no words to express the precise manner in which the Self manifests the various stages of finite consciousness because it is done in 'no manner', that is, without means, or without action involving any effort or lapse of time on the part of the Self. The Self passes into the state of Self-consciousness just as soon as it wills to do so, and no sooner. It is under no necessity to realize, just as it is under no necessity to abandon itself to the finite order, to identify itself with a limited mode of consciousness. In other words, the Self, the infinite Reality, puts itself under the bondage of nescience (*avidya*) and takes the viewpoint of an ego quite freely, and without the slightest loss of its essential infinitude. It is absurd, then, to think that the Self *should* be in some other state of consciousness than that in which it wills to be, that it *ought* to be willing realization instead of the present state of ego-centricity. The Self is in the state in which, as one with the ultimate Reality, it wills to be. In religious language, it is impossible to have the mystical vision unless

[1] *The Huang Po Doctrine of Universal Mind*. Trs. Chu Ch'an (London, 1947), pp. 16 and 24.

God wills it, and thus there is absolutely nothing which can be done by the ego to attain it. On the other hand, the Self has no need to realize because it is never inherently limited or bound.

'We cannot bring about the mystic union in ourselves when God does not give it; anyone can prove to himself that to will it is not sufficient. . . . We plunge ourselves in God only in the precise measure in which he wills it. . . . With the aid of grace it is always within the power of my will to *think* of him, which is ordinary prayer. But it is clear that if I wish really to enter into communication with him, this will is no longer sufficient. *An obstacle must be removed;* and the Divine Hand alone is powerful to accomplish this.'[1]

Or in the words of St. Teresa:

'If (God) makes it clear what place each one is to fill, it would be a strange humility for you to choose for yourself. Leave that to the Master of the house. He is wise, he is powerful, he knows what is best for you and for himself. . . . His judgements are his own—we have no right to interfere with them. It is well the decision does not rest with us, for, thinking it a more peaceful way, we should all immediately become great contemplatives! O, what a gain is ours if, for fear of losing by it, we do not seek to gain by what *we* think is best.'[2]

At first sight this may appear to be a very dismal conclusion. It seems that nothing can be done to advance the coming of realization, and so it remains only to sit and wait, or just go on living in the ordinary way. At second sight, however, the conclusion is perhaps less dismal than exasperating, for it becomes evident that even sitting and waiting is beside the point. Whether one tries to do something or to do nothing about realization, in either instance one is overlooking the truth that both action and inaction involve the error of supposing that realization is something to be attained in the future. But since the content of realization is eternal, it must in some sense be present at this moment. Thus to wait for it denies its presence just as much as seeking for it actively.

It seems, then, that one must simply learn to believe that the Self is one with the infinite, and that one's present state of consciousness is the will of the Self and therefore a perfect expression of the infinite whether this be actually known or not. Be

---

[1] Poulain, *Graces of Interior Prayer*, pp. 115-16.
[2] *Way of Perfection*, xvii. Trs. Zimmerman (London, 1935).

your ordinary self; accept yourself just as you are at this moment; this is the infinite will, and nothing else is required of you. Yet there are at least two objections to this. One is that the very effort to believe in present identity with the infinite, or to accept the present moment of consciousness as it is, still carries the implication that something has to be done about it. To try to believe implies that one really doubts. To seek realization by the expedient of imagining it already present is still seeking, for if it were present it would not be necessary to imagine or believe. The other objection is that such acceptance of the present, such cessation of all seeking and striving and discipline, would make one nothing better than a clod. Ma-tsu, another exponent of Zen, puts the problem thus:

'In the Tao there is nothing to discipline oneself in. If there is any discipline in it, the completion of such discipline means the destruction of the Tao. . . . But if there is no discipline whatever in the Tao, one remains an ignoramus.'[1]

## [ii]

While it is true, from one point of view, that nothing can be done to produce realization, the fact remains that those in whom there is any immediate capacity for realization are not permitted to sit and wait. For as soon as the Self begins to will the end of the ego-conscious stage, the ego becomes inflamed with a passion for God, or for metaphysical knowledge, which it imagines to be of its own choosing. Naturally the immediate motive for this desire will be egoistic, but the ultimate motive is the will of the Self. The very fact that a person begins to be interested in the spiritual life, in realization, in union with God, is a certain sign that the process of awakening has begun and that the phase of evolution has been entered.

It has already been noted that all love whatsoever, however selfish it may be, is ultimately motivated by the divine love. For wherever the Self may be in the cycle of involution and evolution, it is always willing the motion of the cycle to its end and fulfilment. Human life is therefore ordered and directed towards realization as its proper end, and however far one may actually be from it the divine will moves steadily towards it, even though the course may lie downward on the cycle through the most

[1] Suzuki, *Manual of Zen Buddhism* (Kyoto, 1935), p. 126.

difficult and 'evil' passages of ego-consciousness. There is, indeed, nothing merely mechanical in this movement, for though we represent the cycle of involution and evolution by a regular circle, it is in fact a curve of extreme complexity, ever twisting and turning and doubling back upon its path.

Therefore although the ego can do nothing to help or hinder the voluntary awakening of the Self to its true nature, the presence of a motive toward realization in the ego shows that one need not ask *how* to love God. One already loves him. In the words of St. Bernard, 'No one is able to seek Thee, save because he has first found'.[1] However much it may seem that the seeker and the Sought are poles apart, the very existence of the quest signifies an affinity between them. Thus when anyone, for whatever apparent motive, begins to think of God, to practise any spiritual exercise or to desire realization, he is expressing the will of the Self. Were this not so he could neither want nor be able to do it.

It is for this reason that Catholic doctrine has always maintained that true prayer is not simply man relating himself to God, but rather something which God is performing in and through man. Prayer has its origin, not in the soul, but in the indwelling Holy Spirit, and thus prayer is man's participation in the interior life of the Holy Trinity—even in its most stumbling and rudimentary form.

'The consistently characteristic Christian view has been that mere man cannot pray at all, that no movement of desire on the part of the natural man can constitute real prayer. It is God in us that prays. It is our nature penetrated by the divine Spirit, and assisted by the divine grace, that is alone capable of prayer in the full Christian sense.'[2]

This is why Christian worship is the performance of the act of the God-man Christ, the celebration of *his* Eucharist, whereby the Church signifies that it prays as Christ and not as a mere collection of independent human egos.

The emergence of realization is therefore shown by the type of spiritual exercise or by the nature of the spiritual consciousness which the Self permits one to practise and enjoy, or towards which it moves one's desire. The first stage of development is that wherein the Self, still firmly identified with the ego, pro-

[1] *De diligendo Deo*, vii.
[2] Lilley, *Prayer in Christian Theology* (London, 1925), p. 4.

jects itself upon God considered as an external object. If, then, the ego is moved to pray and worship in the ordinary sense, or to meditate upon the divine nature, or simply to contemplate God as the Great Other with silent adoration, it is clear that the first stage has been entered. This stage is, however, peculiarly and essentially religious, for the fact that God is considered as an *object* of knowledge and love indicates that one is in the realm of analogical knowledge, working through reason, feeling and sense.

The next stage begins to assume a definitely metaphysical character because it involves the distinction of the Self from the ego, and the withdrawal of the projected image of God into the knowing subject. Its appearance is indicated by an inclination and ability to let go of the ego and all that pertains to it, an act which may be performed in various ways. Two of these will be considered as the more usual and important, although the first involves certain difficulties which make it hard for people living in modern civilization.

The first way, then, consists in the ability to engage in a particularly intense form of concentration such as is practised in Hindu *yoga*, a concentration which may be developed through Christian prayer as a result of extreme devotion and attention to the external image of God. This has the effect of emptying the field of consciousness of all other objects apart from the point of concentration, so that awareness of the ego simply disappears. Such concentration is not so much a sustained effort as an act of profound relaxation. Preliminary attempts to concentrate are always hindered by countless distractions, but if, as is usual, one endeavours to get rid of them by violence, by forcing them out of mind, the result is only increased turmoil. It is like trying to smooth rough water with a flat-iron. But distractions vanish when the mind is thoroughly relaxed, such relaxation being the object of the various breathing exercises practised in *yoga*, as well as of the special postures of the body which are designed to keep the mind relaxed and alert without going to sleep.

The point of concentration may be a physical or mental image, or a word or phrase repeated over and over, such as the *Pater Noster*, the *Ave Maria*, or simply the Name of God. The Russian *hesychast* prayer, 'Lord Jesus Christ, Son of God, have mercy' is constantly used by Orthodox monks in precisely the same fashion as the practitioner of *yoga* uses the syllable *Om*—the *pranava* or supreme name of *Brahma*.

After some considerable practice the act of concentration becomes almost automatic, and the object takes entire possession of consciousness. In other words, the Self identifies itself with the object of concentration instead of the ego. It ceases to let itself be fascinated by sense-impressions, feelings and thoughts, and instead becomes totally absorbed in one single and simple object. During this time physical actions are continued more or less automatically, as one walks in a dream, and the difficulty of this entire exercise is that it is quite dangerous to become so deeply absorbed unless under the supervision of an experienced director and in the protected surroundings of a monastery.

As a rule the identification of the Self with the object of concentration does not last long. Some internal or external event occurs which suddenly 'shatters' the object, bringing the identification to an abrupt close. And in one intense moment of vision the pure consciousness of the Self, without any object of identification left in the field of awareness, knows itself alone and immediately.

Because of the considerable difficulty and danger of this exercise we have only discussed it sketchily, though there is a vast literature on the subject if anyone should desire to know more about it.[1] The important point to remember is that the entire process of the exercise is willed by the Self rather than the ego. If one cannot, or does not want to, perform it, the Self does not will it.

The second way is far more suited to persons living in the world, and though, like the first, it has its counterpart in the history of Western spirituality, it is specially characteristic of Chinese rather than Hindu tradition.[2] While, like every spiritual exercise, it involves a considerable degree of concentration and clear attention, it does not consist in removing all objects and impressions from consciousness save one. On the contrary, it is

[1] On the *hesychast* prayer, see *The Way of a Pilgrim*. Trs. R. M. French (London, 1941). On oriental methods, see *The Yoga-Sutras of Patanjali*. Trs. M. N. Dvivedi (Madras, 1934). Also Suzuki, *Essays in Zen Buddhism*, Vol. 2, ch. 1 (London, 1933). For a general survey, Tillyard, *Spiritual Exercises* (London, 1927).

[2] China having a colder and less fertile climate than India was not conducive to a purely contemplative spirituality requiring long periods of absence from external consciousness.

the ability to retain one's normal and everyday consciousness and at the same time to let go of it. That is to say, one begins to take an objective view of the stream of thoughts, impressions, feelings and experiences which constantly flows through the mind. Instead of trying to control and interfere with it, one simply lets it flow as it pleases. But whereas consciousness normally lets itself be carried away by the flow, in this case the important thing is to *watch* the flow without being carried away.

In the Chinese metaphysical tradition this is termed *wu-hsin* or 'idealessness', signifying a state of consciousness in which one simply accepts experiences as they come without interfering with them on the one hand or identifying oneself with them on the other. One does not judge them, form theories about them, try to control them, or attempt to change their nature in any way; one lets them be free to be just exactly what they are. 'The perfect man', said Chuang-tzu, 'employs his mind as a mirror; it grasps nothing, it refuses nothing, it receives but does not keep.' This must be quite clearly distinguished from mere empty-mindedness on the one hand, and from ordinary undisciplined mind-wandering on the other.

'The capacity of Mind is wide and great; it is like the emptiness of space. To sit with a mind emptied makes one fall into emptiness of indifference. Space contains the sun, the moon, the stars, constellations, great earth, mountains, and rivers. All grasses and plants, good men and bad men, bad things and good things, heaven and hell—they are all in empty space. The emptiness of (Self-) nature as it is in all people is just like this. (Self-) nature contains in it all objects: *hence* it is great. . . . Seeing all human beings and non-human beings, as they are, evil and good, evil things and good things, it abandons them not, nor is it contaminated with them; it is like the emptiness of space.'[1]

This differs again from ordinary mind-wandering because, as pointed out, the flow of impressions is watched calmly and attentively, but without any kind of criticism.

When this has been kept up for some time, it becomes apparent that there is a ground or inmost centre of consciousness which *always* watches and witnesses the stream of experience in this way, even when we seem to be most absorbed in its turmoil.

[1] Hui-neng's *Tan-ching*, 24 and 25. Trs. D. T. Suzuki, *Manual of Zen Buddhism*, p. 98.

This is, of course, the pure consciousness of the Self which is never really and principially limited by finite experience. But by this spiritual exercise, the Self becomes aware of its principal freedom and distinction from the stream of events and impressions.

It is important to understand that this exercise is much more fundamental than a sort of Stoic detachment from external eventuality. It does not include any attempt to *force* the mind to be calm or to exclude its natural reactions to circumstances. These inner reactions are permitted and *watched* in just the same way as events in the outer world, for by this means the Self is distinguished from the ego-complex of thought and feeling. Thus the Self becomes aware of itself as identical with the infinite all-inclusiveness in which things are free to live and move and have their being, without detracting in any way from its transcendent purity.

Although we have spoken of this state of consciousness as a *distinction* of the Self from the stream of experience, this requires some modification. The Self distinguishes itself from finite experience not by rejecting it but by accepting it, by letting it be free to be as it is. For the infinite is not to be set over against the finite as something existing apart from it, and realization does not therefore consist in *isolating* the Self from the ego and the contents of consciousness. As we have seen, the nature of the Self and of the infinite is precisely *not* to be 'stand-offish', to separate itself from the finite. Therefore the purpose of this particular spiritual exercise is not so much to divide the Self from the stream of experience as to let it accept and include the finite consciously instead of unconsciously. For realization is simply bringing an unconscious process into consciousness.

Thus in the unconscious and ego-conscious stages the Self, as one with the infinite, always wills that which it experiences as a finite point of view. In realization this process becomes conscious. It becomes conscious when you, as the Self, find yourself able to will or accept your total experience, your state of mind and being as it is at any moment. This is something wholly different from lying down inertly under the heel of an impersonal Fate. It is the understanding that you, in identity with the infinite Self, are just exactly what you will to be and have just those experiences which you will to experience. Because of this Supreme Identity of the Self and the infinite, of the will of the

Self and the will of the infinite, you accept and affirm *in clear consciousness* all that you are, all that you do, and all that you know and feel.

There is no question of *how* to do this. Consciously or unconsciously, the Self is doing it all the time. If you are conscious of it, this is realization. If you are not conscious of it, you can try to be by trying to do it. In the attempt you will see quite clearly that the ego cannot do it, and this clear perception of the limitations of the ego will awaken you to the Self, to the fact that it is the Self which perceives those limitations. But if the Self does not as yet will realization, such trial will be either impossible or merely confusing.

To describe the entire undertaking in a rather different way, the letting go or acceptance of your experience and state of mind as it is, is always the act of living completely and perfectly in *this moment*. For we have noted that ego-consciousness is a bondage to time, being essentially a complex of memories and anticipations. All ego-centric action has an eye to the past or the future; in the strict present the ego does not exist. This is easier to prove by experiment rather than by theory, for in concentrating simply and solely upon what is happening at this moment, memory, anticipation and anxiety vanish. Consciousness of this moment is pure awareness without any admixture of phantasy, for past and future are real only when they are present. To live in the past or for the future, which is the general practice of the ego, is to live in unreality, to bind oneself in a chain of dreams. Because the present is a sizeless, infinitesimal point, there is no room in it for the ego. It is the straight and narrow gate which leadeth unto life. In the infinitesimal there is room only for the infinite, wherefore the consciousness of each moment is the pure awareness of the Self. Yet by the paradox of non-duality, which is that the infinite does not exclude the finite, the entire universe exists nowhere but in this sizeless and timeless present moment.

As the infinite consciousness of *Brahma* comprehends all the events of time in the 'one moment' of eternity, so the Self, the *atma*, comprehends simply and solely what is happening at *this* moment of time. The difference between *Brahma* and *atma* is the difference between the infinite and the infinitesimal; essentially they are one. It is for this reason, then, that he who realizes the *atma*, he who is Self-conscious, has no anxiety for the morrow,

TIME

for as the *atma* is the projection of *Brahma*, living in the present is the projection of living in eternity.

Many masters of the spiritual life have therefore laid especial value upon the exercise of living and thinking simply in this moment, letting the past and future drop out of mind; for the ego drops away with them, together with its pride in the past and its fear and greed for the future. When this has been practised for some time, it will become apparent, as before, that in actual reality it is impossible to live outside this moment. Obviously our thoughts of past and future transpire in the present, and in this sense it is impossible to concentrate on anything except what is happening now. However, by *trying* to live simply in the present, by trying to cultivate the pure 'momentary' awareness of the Self, we discover in experience as well as theory that the attempt is unnecessary. We learn that never for an instant has the time-thinking of the ego actually interfered with the eternal and momentary consciousness of the Self. Underlying memory, anticipation, anxiety and greed there has always been this centre of pure and unmoved awareness, which never at any time departed from present reality, and was therefore never actually bound by the chain of dreams.

The first step, then, is to concentrate attention simply upon present experience, temporarily, therefore, suspending memory and anticipation. By this means we understand experimentally that in the pure present there is no egotism. The next step is the realization that it is in fact impossible to place attention anywhere apart from the present. As soon as this is actually realized it becomes possible once more to entertain memory and anticipation, and yet be free from their binding power. For as soon as one is able to look upon memory and anticipation as present, one has made them (and the ego which they constitute) objective. Formerly they were subjective, because they consisted in *identifying oneself* with past or future events, that is, with the temporal chain constituting the ego. But when one is able, for instance, to regard anticipation as present, one is no longer identifying oneself with the future, and is therefore taking the viewpoint of the Self as distinct from the ego. To put it in another way: as soon as the ego's act of identifying itself with the future can be seen as something present, one is seeing it from a standpoint superior to the ego, from the standpoint of the Self.

It follows that when our centre of consciousness has shifted to the strictly present and momentary outlook of the Self, memory and anticipation become quite peripheral and objective actions of the mind, and our being is no more dominated by and identified with the egoistic mode of thought. We have all the serenity, all the keen awareness, all the freedom from temporality, of one who lives wholly in the present, and yet without the absurd limitation of not being able to remember the past or to provide for the future. Realization of the Self is thus the realization of an eternal and inescapable *Presence*. In the words of a famous passage from Emerson's *Essay on Self-Reliance*:

'These roses under my window make no reference to former roses or to better ones; they are for what they are; they exist with God to-day. There is no time to them. There is simply the rose; it is perfect in every moment of its existence. . . . But man postpones or remembers; he does not live in the present, but with reverted eye laments the past, or, heedless of the riches that surround him, stands on tiptoe to foresee the future. He cannot be happy and strong until he too lives with nature in the present, above time.'

It will by now be clear that all these spiritual exercises are attempts to do what is already being done. By trying to conform to the divine will, we discover that it is impossible to escape from it. By trying to release and accept the stream of experience, we find that our inmost consciousness never does anything else. By trying to live in the timeless and ego-less eternal now, we learn that in truth we have always been living in it. Herein lies the most important principle of realization, which is to understand that our Supreme Identity with the infinite Self is best known not in looking for it, but in accepting the truth of its *inescapable* reality and presence. As with the living moment, the more you try to grasp and stay it, the more it flees; yet in fact you cannot get out of it.

*It is only when you seek it that you lose.*
*You cannot take hold of it, nor can you get rid of it.*[1]

This will explain the constant references in Zen literature to the truth that realization is 'your everyday thoughts', that 'usual life is the Tao', that 'the everyday mind is the true law', or that 'act as you will, go on as you feel, this is the Incomparable Way'—for whether one is enlightened or ignorant there is in

[1] *Cheng-tao Ke*, 34. Suzuki, *Manual of Zen*, p. 115.

reality no escape from the Supreme Identity nor from perfect harmony with the Tao or the infinite will.

'The alternation of the passive and active principles is called the Tao. From the result (of their alternation) comes goodness, for herein is manifested the completeness of nature. Benevolent men see it and call it benevolence. Wise men see it and call it wisdom. Ordinary people act daily in accordance with it, but do not know it. Thus the Tao as seen by the superior man is seen by few.'[1]

The nearest equivalent to this kind of thing in Western religion is the practice so much advocated by de Caussade and Dom John Chapman of affirming and accepting every experience that comes to us as the will of God.[2] Obviously the metaphysical order of acceptance goes far beyond this, because religion in its necessary confusion of Self and ego must regard an identity of the will of the Self and the will of God as both dangerous and absurd. Indeed, its relative danger is not at all to be underestimated, for there is nothing 'safe' about the preparations for realization, and no one should undertake them without being ready to face the most serious risks. When anything of this kind is attempted without the clearest distinction of the Self from the ego, the danger of individualism and antinomianism is ever present.

For this reason the exercise requires careful attention to the *order* in which the stream of events is accepted. Invariably an external action which, from the moral standpoint, is sin, is the result of *not* accepting some *prior* state of the soul, whether of insecurity, boredom, frustration or anger. The external sin is an attempt to escape from an internal limitation, and if the internal limitations are thoroughly accepted, the external escape will not be required. Therefore to neglect the acceptance of the prior internal states of the soul, to refuse to *let be* the discomfort and the pain and the fear from which sin is the attempted escape, is to fail totally in performing the exercise. This is not to say that

[1] *I Ching*, Appendix iii, i. v.

[2] 'Every moment is the message of God's will; every external event, everything outside us, and *even every involuntary thought and feeling within us* is God's own touch. We are living in touch with God. Everything we come in contact with, the whole of our daily circumstances, and all our interior responses, whether pleasures or pains, are God's working.' Dom John Chapman, *Spiritual Letters* (London, 1944), p. 143.

the moral point of view is in any way absolute, but simply that ego-centric activity implies that one is still ego-conscious and not at all Self-conscious.

While the second of these two ways of spiritual practice does not involve the difficult and sometimes dangerous mono-ideism, the intense concentration on one exclusive point, which is characteristic of the first, it does involve considerable clarity of attention and mental relaxation. It is therefore greatly aided by all those spiritual disciplines which tend to relax the mind and clear the consciousness, such as regularity of external life, deep and rhythmic control of the breath, avoidance of nervous agitation, the cultivation—if possible—of quiet surroundings, and proper attention to the health of the body. These matters are useful rather than essential, for there are persons who have been able to practise this way of life despite the most trying external conditions. It always remains true that the essential consciousness proper to the Self does not need to be calmed or cleared, or to be made to accept the stream of impressions, but this does not become conscious until one has tried to make it so.

When the Self is thus 'distinguished' from the ego, no further exercise is needed to make it aware of its *principal* identity with the infinite. This simply becomes self-evident, for its light shines and does not need to illumine itself. But, even when realization has come to pass, so long as the field of its consciousness is allowed to be occupied predominantly with the life and affairs of the ego, the omni-consciousness proper to the infinite is not resumed.[1]

It will now be clear from what has been said that the term 'realization' is used for the attainment of metaphysical knowledge, because it is not so much the creation of a new state of affairs as the bringing to consciousness of an eternal state. Realization is the Self emerging from its own voluntary 'slumber' of complete identification with a finite point of view, and it occurs at the moment when one finds oneself able to will and consciously accept the precise point at which one stands on the cycle of life. For this constitutes a consciousness of perfect harmony between one's own and the divine will, and the further discovery that the two are one. The ego as such can never make this discovery because it can no more accept itself and its place on the cycle than a musical instrument can play itself. However,

[1] See above, p. 151 ff.

the very fact that man, as an ego, can *attempt* to accept or to know himself is the certain sign that he is more than ego and is beginning to realize it.

The following Hindu parable expresses most aptly the concurrence of realization with the total acceptance of one's place on the cycle. There were two sages meditating in the forest, the one plunged in such profound mental stillness that moss and cobwebs covered his immobile body, and the other dancing round a tree, singing the praises of God. One day Krishna, who had descended from heaven, came through the forest, and the compelling power of his divine presence awakened the first sage from his trance. At once he recognized who Krishna was, and called out:

'O Krishna, when you return to heaven will you please ask the Supreme Brahma how long it will take me to attain realization, and then come back and tell me?'

Krishna consented to this request, and passing on to the second sage was asked the same favour. At this he ascended into the highest heaven, consulted with the Supreme Brahma, and returned again to earth.

Recognizing him again, the first sage asked eagerly, 'O Krishna, have you been back to heaven and seen the Supreme Brahma? And did he tell you how long it would take me to attain realization?'

'Indeed I did', answered Krishna, 'and the Supreme Brahma told me that it would take you but three more lives upon the wheel of birth and death, and thereafter realization will be yours.'

But at this the sage began to moan and complain, 'These many years, these many lives, these many aeons have I struggled to attain, practising the most rigid austerities and the most profound meditations! Must I abide yet three more long lives of discipline and suffering and effort?'

And he sank into black despair. Krishna therefore passed on to the second sage, and to his question gave this reply:

'The Supreme Brahma has told me to tell you that before realization can be yours, you will have to live as many lives as there are leaves upon the tree about which you dance.'

The sage looked up into the tree and mused, 'That tree must carry about ten thousand leaves.'

And then, turning to Krishna, he cried, 'You mean that in

only ten thousand more lives I shall really and truly attain realization? O how can I thank you for telling me! Only just ten thousand more! I am so happy!'

At this there came a great voice from heaven, saying:

'My son, you have attained realization at this moment!'

## [iii]

Despite the fact that the realm of spiritual experience is so often described in Christianity as the *interior* life, and that the unanimous testimony of mystical and metaphysical tradition in every part of the world is that 'the Beyond is within', that God is to be found in the deepest and innermost reaches of consciousness, our religion is so largely 'extraverted' that the way of realization as we have described it must necessarily seem strange. In general the religious mind looks *up* to God and devotes itself to him as the *object* of human life, with the feeling that the divine being and the innermost depths of man's consciousness are discontinuous. The very word 'contemplation' as it is used in Christian theology carries the implication of man, as knower and perceiver, gazing *at* God as a totally objective Vision. The imagery of heaven implies that the saints and angels surround God as an object of adoration external to themselves.

Fundamentally, however, all such imagery, all such externalism, is a projection.

'Spirit is never an object; nor is spiritual reality an objective one. In the so-called objective world there is no such nature, thing, or objective reality as spirit. Hence it is easy to deny the reality of spirit. God is spirit because he is not object, because he is subject. . . . In objectification there are no primal realities, but only symbols. The objective spirit is merely a symbolism of spirit. Spirit is realistic while culture and social life are symbolical. In the object there is never any reality, but only the symbol of reality. The subject alone always has reality.'[1]

The symbolism of religion holds, therefore, if it is transposed, if God is considered as the interior rather than exterior centre around which his creatures revolve. Man as finite, as a creature of reason, feeling and sense, revolves about the central Self, and is subordinate to that Self as to God.

The external projection of God is, of course, necessary to the

[1] Berdyaev, *Spirit and Reality* (New York, 1939), pp. 5 and 53.

ego-centric type of consciousness, but that this point of view is in no way final is suggested by the curious fact that the contemplation of God as an external object involves the virtual annihilation of the finite universe. For if the supreme goal of man's life is, as the hymn expresses it,

> 'Prostrate before Thy throne to lie,
> And gaze and gaze on Thee,'

it is impossible to see how, in such a vision, the finite order can have any other function than as a point from which to gaze. Practically speaking, the finite order is simply forgotten, and thus virtually annihilated, in the all-consuming, all-outshining glory of God. In other words, if God be put on the same objective plane as other people, other things, and the whole stupendous and marvellous order of stars, mountains, skies, plants and animals, the light of God will totally out-dazzle and obliterate the rest. The finite order will therefore lose any eternal significance, for to project God into the realm of objects is ultimately to destroy every other object. If God could be an object of reason, feeling or sense, one could think nothing else, feel nothing else and sense nothing else. The universe would dissolve in celestial fire.

Such a consummation contradicts the fundamental Christian intuiton that the finite order has an eternal meaning, and that heaven is a state in which one meets not only God but also his glorified creatures. This contradiction is only resolvable metaphysically, for in realization the knowledge of God is subjective, and therefore does not conflict with the objective world but shines out upon it. The God within illuminates the finite, but the God without destroys it.

It is natural, therefore, that when God is sought from the ego-conscious standpoint, the world is denied. God is sought as an object apart from other objects, and separated thus from his world the latter loses its being. Similarly, if the Self is separated from everyday experience, if it is sought or clung to as an object, a state of mind or feeling, apart from the stream of finite life, it becomes exclusive. It becomes one term of a dualism which excludes the other term. Strictly speaking, however, the subjective and the objective are not opposed; the former includes the latter and does not contest place with it. But the ego-conscious viewpoint opposes the two, setting up I against It and Thou. Therefore ego-consciousness must either love the world to the exclusion of God, or God to the exclusion of the world; there cannot be room for both on the objective plane.

To put it in another way, if God or the Self is sought as an object apart from the world, God's love is denied. God is made into a self-isolating or 'stand-offish' being, and his creation dissolves into nothing. But if God is known as within man's subjective life, as the source and ground of consciousness, he can love and illumine the finite world through man. The divine and human consciousness are found to be continuous, and the infinite and finite orders are no longer opposed and mutually exclusive. The former is the conscious continuum which embraces the latter.

It is clear enough that when the ego makes the love of the world its life-goal, God vanishes and without him the world is found to be mere frustration and dead ashes. So too, when the ego loves God as its object, there comes the opposite extreme of negative religion, excessive asceticism, and world-flight. Thus the ego must learn to love God as its subject and the world as object. The discovery of God as the Self, as the ground of man's consciousness, offers the only true reconciliation of those two great poles of religion represented by theocentric mysticism on the one hand, and the active life of divine charity towards external humanity on the other. Theology begins to express this truth whenever it hints that in the Beatific Vision the glorified universe is seen as *within* God. For the objective is within the subjective, and in realization the external world is known as within the all-embracing consciousness of the Self.

'On the threshold of the most profound and ultimate depths we are faced with the revelation that our experience is contained within the depths of the Divine life itself. But at this point silence reigns, for no human language or concept can express this experience. That is the *apophatic* sphere of irreconcilable contradictions baffling human thought. That is the ultimate realm of free and purified spirituality, which no monistic system is capable of defining. On *this side* there remain dualism, tragedy, conflict, man's dialogue with God, the plural world confronted with the One. It is not by discarding the principle of personality that the absolutely Divine One can be attained, but rather by exploring the spiritual depths of the personality which is antinomically united to the One.'[1]

[1] Berdyaev, *Spirit and Reality*, pp. 198-9.

Because the infinite transcends all dualism, it is able to include dualism, so that realization is in no way incompatible with everyday awareness of the objective world, with physical life and activity. The profound detachment of the Self from the ego and the world is not a detachment of rejection but of acceptance and love. True detachment from things consists in letting them be free to be themselves, which is to say, in not confusing them with the Self. They are confused with the Self when identified with it unconsciously, and when separated from it as if it were an object like themselves. To seek God or the Self as an object of knowledge is to deny the transcendence of the infinite by putting it in the class of objects.

Transcendence is not separation, and similarly, from the metaphysical standpoint, holiness is not 'set-apart-ness' but the wholeness of that which is all-inclusive. It is thus, then, that realization comes through a conscious and deliberate plunging into life, not in retreat from it; through a generous acceptance of finite experience, not in blotting it out of mind; through utter willingness to be what one is, not in trying to lift oneself to heaven by one's own boot-straps. The Self realizes freedom from the finite world by deliberate self-abandonment to its limitations. Thus when asked how to escape the raging heat of finite pain, the Zen master Sozan answered:

'Escape into the midst of the boiling waters, into the midst of a blazing coal.'

In other words, the process of realization is the same as the process of creation and manifestation. The finite order comes into being because the infinite accepts its limitations and abandons itself to it. This is why any attempt to produce realization by artifice is profoundly irrelevant. It is what Zen describes as 'adding frost over snow' or 'putting legs on a snake'. The realization process is going on all the time, or, to speak more correctly, it is eternal. However, when man as the ego attempts to will this process and to accept his limitations, he discovers that the artifice is unnecessary, that he is trying to do what his deepest consciousness is doing already, and thereat his 'centre of gravity' shifts from the ego to the Self. He becomes what he is by the artifice of trying to be what he is. He wills his total experience at this moment, and finds that it is not himself that wills, but God willing it in him. He surrenders himself without reserve to this moment's experience as the will of God, and through surrender discovers perfect freedom. He learns the identity of the divine will with his own, and through that certainty of eternal union with the infinite Reality is delivered from the necessity to sin, from the pride and fear of the ego.

In short, when expressed in language the way of realization is pure paradox. Willingness to be insecure is the ultimate security. Willingness to suffer is the essence of divine joy. Willingness to be finite is to know one's own infinity. Willingness to be a slave is to be truly free. Willingness to be a fool and a sinner is to be both a sage and a saint. This is the mystery of that sacrifice whereby the world is both created and redeemed, 'of the Lamb slain from the foundation of the world'.

It is of course impossible from the ego-conscious standpoint of religion to grasp this basic identity of creation and redemption, to equate redemption with any 'mere realization' of the true nature and meaning of existence. For religion, redemption is an external and transforming intervention in the course of the universe because God is regarded as an external object. This is why religion is always in danger of absolute dualism, for in making so profound a gulf between the power whereby God creates and maintains the universe, and the power whereby he redeems it, religion runs the risk of equating the creative God with the demonic Demiurge. Thus religion will criticize realization as an acceptance of the universe which fails to transform it.

We have already explained why realization proposes no transformation of the finite *by violence*, because its nature is to love and not hate limitation. The entire chaos of the Western world springs from this radical separation of creation and redemption, prompting the technological attempt to transform nature by violent alteration. To divide the creative power from the redemptive power is to demonize the creative. But realization involves more than knowledge of creation's true nature. It involves also the conscious objectivization of that nature—the creative and external expression of the Self in the finite order. When this occurs consciously instead of unconsciously, the expression of the Self has a unitive instead of separative character. Society is given a traditional and cosmological form because it is ordered to its true centre. It is transformed from within outwards, and so assumes the hierarchical nature of a real organism. It is not transformed surgically, from without inwards, so as to heal the symptoms instead of the causes of disorder. It grows out from the centre of metaphysical realization, from its spiritual leadership, as petals grow from a stem. Violent transformation proposes the unnatural monstrosity of plucking the petals from their original stem, and gluing them to an altogether new stem by their outside tips!

But realization heals the social order profoundly by overcoming the root causes of separative and evil action, and by giving outward expression to the hitherto unconscious unity of life—a unity grounded in the fact that God is man's interior and not exterior centre. Realization heals ('makes whole') society organically, working from the inmost spring of its life, drawing a new and invigorating sap from its nethermost roots. But egoconscious activism can only attempt to heal the social order artificially, by surgical rearrangement of its disordered parts, by dictatorial imposition of a purely superficial order which does nothing to correct the true and inward origins of social chaos.

It is not surprising, then, that the Western world has never really understood the nature of spiritual authority, having almost invariably confused it with the external and compulsive power of a secular monarchy. The Church has never effectively realized its organic nature because it has projected its centre of authority outwards without any real recognition that external authority is no more than a symbol of the internal Spirit. It has confused subjective authority with the so-called 'subjectivism' of religious individualism, which is not truly subjective at all. On the contrary, it is a form of myopic objectivism, in which the subject is confused with the objects nearest to it, that is, with the feelings and emotions of the ego, and with the opinions of the individual reason.

With very rare exceptions, that which is truly subjective and interior has thus far remained entirely hidden from Western man. It has been projected wholly upon the objective and external world. The historical Incarnation is, of course, confessedly and necessarily external, because it is God's own projection of himself into history, and is clearly understood by Christian theology to be *the* symbol and analogy of God in terms of time and space. But Western man has projected externally the very spiritual reality which the Incarnation already represents externally, which is redundant to say the least. The God externalized in Christ exists within the centre rather than beyond the outer boundary of our consciousness. This cannot possibly be understood so long as Western man remains unconscious of his inner being, of the truly subjective realm. While such unconsciousness lasts he will, of course, be unable to distinguish the subjective character of oriental metaphysic from extremely introverted ego-centricity.[1] The modern psychology of the unconscious may indeed be the dim dawn of his awakening, and it is possible that in the work of C. G. Jung we have even caught a glimpse of the sun. The very use of the term 'the unconscious' for the inmost depths reveals how little Western man knows of what is actually his central consciousness.

It is, of course, important to remember that in speaking of the spiritual and the subjective as *internal*, the word is not used in a spatial sense, as if God were located inside the human body. The word simply indicates the manner in which God is known, immediately and subjectively rather than mediately and objec-

[1] A striking example of this inability is Maritain's essay 'The Natural Mystical Experience and the Void', in *Ransoming the Time* (New York, 1941). The title is itself a tremendous begging of the question, because there are no solid grounds at all for calling Hindu realization a *natural* experience as distinct from the *supernatural* experience of the Christian mystics. Apparently Maritain thinks it natural because possible to produce by the personal effort of *yoga*, whereas the Christian experience is solely the gift of God, for which the soul can only prepare. This is to introduce a distinction between *yoga* and Christian mystical theology which simply does not exist. The Vedanta, as we have shown, involves no such idea as producing realization by one's own effort or action. (Cf. the quotation from Shankara, p. 181 above.) Maritain goes on to suggest that what is experienced in oriental mysticism is the *esse* of the soul rather than God, presupposing an absolute discontinuity between the *esse* or being of man and the being of God—which is natural enough in Thomism where God is always the *object* of love and knowledge. Furthermore, Maritain seems to be familiar only with the mono-ideistic type of *yoga* which excludes everything from consciousness other than the point of concentration. But mono-ideism is as much a Christian as a Hindu practice, and furthermore is never anything but a preparatory means. *Moksha* itself, the supreme spiritual state of *yoga*, is an inclusive and not at all an exclusive state of consciousness, and is in no sense, as Maritain suggests, a purely negative experience which, because of the identity of negatives, cannot be properly distinguished from a negatively described God. One is tempted to wonder, too, how a philosophy can know anything about the *esse* of the soul when it is so heavily committed to the principle *nihil est in intellectu quod non prius fuerit in sensu*.

tively, because of the continuity of the consciousness in man with the divine. The hint of this truth is already in St. Augustine's remark that 'our spirit is heaven, our flesh earth',[1] from which it would follow that the Father in heaven is the subjective Spirit. Thus the way of realization is summed up in the prayer, 'Thy will be done on earth as it is in heaven'. For realization is bringing to consciousness, to earth, what is true all the time in the 'unconscious', in the Self and spirit which the ego does not know. From the eternal and interior standpoint, that is, in heaven, the divine will is always done, but this has yet to be realized from the finite, temporal and external standpoint of earth.

'Thy kingdom come, thy will be done on earth as it is in heaven,' sums up, too, the whole meaning of the great act of incarnation and self-abandonment whereby the infinite manifests the finite. It is that God, the ultimate Reality, who knows himself in eternity wills to realize himself in time, and who knows himself in the unity and simplicity of the infinite wills to realize himself in the multiplicity and complexity of the finite. That this realization is the work of God and not of man, of the Self and not of the ego, is the reason why 'Thy will be done' is no resolution but a prayer.

It is an inevitability of language and thought that all ideas of God, the infinite, and the Self suggest some object apart from other objects, some *thing* to be known apart from other things. Even when it is understood that the infinite includes and embraces the realm of known objects, there is still the idea of some sort of large thing containing all small things. In the same way, it is inevitable that realization be conceived as some state of mind or feeling different and apart from other states, and especially from whatever state is ours at this present moment. To avoid this impression, it is often said in metaphysical doctrine that the infinite simply *is* the finite, and that realization is nothing other than one's present state of mind. Yet even this cannot avoid the inherent dualism of thought. On the one hand, to say that the infinite is the finite is to create an artificial redundance by uniting two things which in reality are not two at all, and thus in no need of union. On the other hand, it sounds like the most crass pantheism—which is equally wide of the

[1] *Sermo*, lviii. Cf. also, *De Dono Perseverentiae*, iii, 6: 'Vult autem ille doctor et martyr coelum et terram intelligi spiritum et carnem.'

mark, because, as we have tried to show, to say that the infinite and the finite are not two is *not* to say that they are simply and numerically one.[1]

This is why Zen prefers to indicate the ultimate Reality without conceptual language, seeking a more direct mode of expression than circuitous and negative terminology borrowed from philosophy. More than enough has been said to show that realization cannot be communicated by any amount of explanation and theory. If there is any way of communicating realization from one mind to another, we believe that the nearest approach to an adequate method is this peculiar 'direct pointing' of Zen, which has been of such profound fascination to all who have given it serious attention. In the mere twenty or thirty years since a knowledge of Zen has been available in the West, it has been recognized as employing a unique methodology of spiritual instruction.[2]

To those unfamiliar with the typical procedure of Zen instruction, the following instance may be illuminating.

'A scholar said to Hogen, "When I was studying under Seiho, I got an idea as to the truth of Zen."

' "What is your understanding, then?" asked Hogen.

' "When I asked the master who was the Buddha (i.e. what is Reality), he said, 'Ping-ting comes for fire'."

' "It's a fine answer", said Hogen, "but probably you misunderstand it. Let me see how you take the meaning of it."

' "Well" explained the scholar, "Ping-ting is the god of fire; when he himself comes for fire, it is like myself, who, being a Buddha from the very beginning, wants to know who the Buddha (or the Self) is. No questioning is then needed, as I am already the Buddha himself."

' "There!" exclaimed Hogen. "Just as I thought! You are completely off. Now you ask me."

' "Who is the Buddha?"

[1] Cf. Sozan's *Shinjin-no-mei*, 25:

> 'In the higher realm of true Suchness
> There is neither "self" nor "other":
> When direct identification is sought,
> We can only say, "Not two".'
>
> Suzuki, *Manual of Zen Buddhism*, p. 96.

[2] Readers of my former works will be familiar enough with examples of the Zen method. For a full discussion see my *The Way of Zen* (New York, 1957).

' "Ping-ting comes for fire".'[1]

Puzzling as this interchange may seem to be at first sight, prolonged thought will only make it the more difficult to understand. The more you look through the drawers, under the bed and bureau, in the closet and on the bathroom shelf for the spectacles you are already wearing, the further you will be from finding them. According to Zen, the point of the story is as self-evident as it can be, just as there is nothing more totally obvious and fundamentally self-evident than the infinite Reality in whose consciousness and being we live and move. Our trouble is that the egoistic viewpoint is so thoroughly complex that it has extreme difficulty in recognizing the essentially simple.

The entire point of the Zen method is therefore to draw attention to the absolute self-evidence of the ultimate Reality. For though it is 'nearer than breathing' and 'closer than hands and feet', we expend untold effort in seeking it as something wholly obscure and remote. Nothing is therefore of more importance in the work of realization than to remember that what you desire to know is simple rather than complex, present rather than absent, obvious rather than hidden. Many are the dead ends, the pitfalls of spiritual pride, the fruitless researches and sorry disappointments avoided by recollection of this principle. If anything, the words 'simple, present and obvious' are too weak to describe the radical self-evidence and the instant immediacy of the infinite Self.

In Zen one of the favourite ways of expressing realization is the use of a certain kind of poetry. As may be expected, the precise way in which this indicates the ultimate, non-dual Reality is at once so subtle and simple that any attempt at explanation is redundant and confusing. This use of poetry does not, as we might imagine, involve any recourse to analogy or symbolism. On the contrary, it is about as direct an expression of Reality as is possible.

> 'Through the evening mist
> A lone goose is flying.
> Of one tone
> Are wide waters and sky.'[2]

---

[1] After Suzuki, *Essays in Zen*, i. (London, 1927), p. 294.
[2] From the *Zenrin* collection. Trs. Sokei-an Sasaki, in *Cat's Yawn* (New York, 1947), p. 58.

The symbolist will detect in the lone goose a representation of the finite object, and in the one tone of waters and sky the infinite continuum in which it is manifest. From the aesthetic viewpoint, it may be thought that this suggests that solitary misty mood which is imagined to be the highest flight of Taoist contemplation. Such interpretations are completely off the mark. The poem expresses realization so clearly that any symbolical elaboration wraps it in a veil. As for any identification of realization with a 'solitary misty mood', where is any such aestheticism in this:

> 'To tread the sharp edge of a sword;
> To run on smooth-frozen ice,
> One needs no footsteps to follow.
> Walk over the cliffs with hands free.'[1]

To grasp the meaning of these expressions one must understand them immediately as they come to pure consciousness, before there has been time to think anything or feel anything about them.

> 'Lightning flashes,
> Sparks shower.
> In one blink of your eyes
> You have missed seeing.'[2]

Not only the poems, but life as we know it at this and every moment of the eternal Now is to be understood in the same way. This, then, is the final word that needs no further comment:

> 'Through the evening mist
> A lone goose is flying.
> Of one tone
> Are wide waters and sky.'

[1] *Wu-men-kan*, xxxii. Trs. Senzaki and Reps, *The Gateless Gate* (Los Angeles, 1934), p. 51.
[2] Ibid., p. 36.

# BIBLIOGRAPHY

The following is a carefully selected list of works on oriental metaphysic for the guidance of readers who wish to pursue the subject more deeply. Students of comparative religions may be surprised at the omission of certain 'standard' works, for we have been at pains to include only those which do not seriously misrepresent their subject.

BLOFELD, JOHN (Trs.). *The Path to Sudden Attainment*. A Treatise of the Ch'an (Zen) School of Chinese Buddhism, by Hui Hai of the T'ang Dynasty (London, 1948).

CHU CH'AN (Trs.). *The Huang Po Doctrine of Universal Mind*. Being the teaching of Dhyana Master Hsi Yun (London, 1947). One of the best and most authoritative of original sources on the teaching and practice of Zen Buddhism, and the metaphysic of the Mahayana in general.

CH'U TA-KAO (Trs.). *The Tao Te Ching* (London, 1937). Of the many translations of this work, this is probably the best that has been done since the original, and regrettably unobtainable, French version by Stanislas Julien. It is also included in its entirety in Robert Ballou's *Bible of the World* (New York, 1939).

COOMARASWAMY, ANANDA K. *Am I My Brother's Keeper?* (New York, 1947). An admirable collection of short essays on the spiritual and cultural relations of East and West, including an appreciation of the work of René Guénon.

*Figures of Speech or Figures of Thought?* (Luzac and Co., London, 1946).

*Hinduism and Buddhism* (New York, 1943). An excellent introduction to their comparative mythology and doctrine, and one of the few works which relates Buddhism correctly to its Hindu origins.

*Recollection, Indian and Platonic* (New Haven, 1944).

*Religious Basis of the Forms of Indian Society* (New York, 1946).

*Time and Eternity* (Ascona, 1947). A profound and well-documented study of the subject according to Hindu, Buddhist, Greek, Islamic and Christian traditions.

# BIBLIOGRAPHY

DVIVEDI, M. N. (Trs.). *Mandukyopanishad*. With Gaudapada's Karikas and the Bhashya of Shankara (Bombay, 1909).

*The Yoga-Sutras of Patanjali* (Madras, 1934). A good translation, with Sanskrit text, despite a certain Theosophical bias in the commentary.

EDGERTON, FRANKLIN (Trs.). *The Bhagavad-Gita*. 2 vols. With Sanskrit text (Harvard, 1944).

EVANS-WENTZ, W. Y. (Trs.). *Tibetan Yoga and Secret Doctrines* (London, 1935).

*The Tibetan Book of the Dead* (Oxford, 1957).

*The Tibetan Book of the Great Liberation*. Foreword by C. G. Jung (Oxford, 1954).

GILES, H. A. (Trs.). *Chuang Tzu* (London and Shanghai, 1926). This is the standard translation of this excellent and profoundly humorous exponent of Taoism. The translator's commentary is weak. See also under Lin Yutang.

GILES, LIONEL (Trs.). *Taoist Teachings* (Wisdom of the East Series, London, 1925). An anthology of writings attributed to Lieh-tzu, who, after Lao-tzu and Chuang-tzu, is the third most important exponent of Taoism.

GUENON, RENE. *The Crisis of the Modern World*. Trs. Arthur Osborne (Luzac and Co., London, 1942). The predicament of a world order bereft of metaphysical knowledge.

*East and West*. Trs. William Massey (Luzac and Co., London, 1941). The basic differences in oriental and modern occidental points of view. Should be read as an introduction to the above.

*Introduction to the Study of the Hindu Doctrines*. Trs. Marco Pallis (Luzac and Co., London, 1945). Quite the most admirable introduction available.

*Man and His Becoming According to the Vedanta*. Trs. Richard C. Nicholson (Luzac and Co., London, 1945). Read as a sequel to the *Introduction*, this is a most comprehensive and reliable summary of the Vedanta.

*Autorité spirituelle et Pouvoir temporel* (Paris, 1930).

*Les Etats Multiples de l' Etre* (Paris, 1932).

*La Métaphysique orientale* (Paris, 1946).

*La Règne de la Quantité et les Signes des Temps* (Paris, 1945).

HUME, ROBERT E. (Trs.). *The Thirteen Principal Upanishads*

# BIBLIOGRAPHY

(Oxford University Press, 1921).

LIN YUTANG (Ed. and Trs.). *The Wisdom of China and India* (New York, 1942). A useful anthology of oriental texts— Hindu, Buddhist, Taoist and Confucian—including excerpts from the *Upanishads,* the *Bhagavad-Gita,* the *Yogasutra,* the *Surangma Sutra,* and the editor's own translations of Lao-tzu and Chuang-tzu.

*The Wisdom of Laotse* (New York, 1948). A marvellous translation which has the special advantage of using large selections from Chuang Tzu as a commentary.

MASCARO, JUAN (Trs.). *Himalayas of the Soul.* Translations from the Sanskrit of the Principal Upanishads (John Murray, London, 1938).

McGOVERN, WILLIAM. *Introduction to Mahayana Buddhism* (Kegan Paul and Co., London, 1922). Probably the best of the very few works giving a general survey of the Mahayana.

NIKHILANANDA, SWAMI (Trs.). *Self-Knowledge* (New York, 1947). This is a translation of Shankara's *Atma Bodha,* together with a long introduction on the nature of the Vedanta by the translator.

NORTHROP, F. S. C. *The Meeting of East and West* (New York, 1946). Notable for its perception of the unity of the spiritual traditions of the Orient, and for a brilliantly thought-provoking discussion of the relations between East and West in every sphere of life.

PRABHAVANANDA, SWAMI, and MANCHESTER, F. (Trs.). *The Upanishads* (Hollywood, 1947). A convenient and readable translation of the principal *Upanishads.*

PRATT, JAMES B. *The Pilgrimage of Buddhism* (New York, 1928). A monumental work covering the entire field of Buddhism, ancient and modern.

RADHAKRISHNAN, S. *The Philosophy of the Upanishads* (G. Allen and Unwin, London, 1924). Despite some minor defects, this book clears up many common misapprehensions about the doctrine of the *Upanishads,* especially those disseminated by the German school.

REPS, PAUL (Ed.) *Zen Flesh, Zen Bones* (Rutland, Vt., 1957). A readable, though sometimes inexact, translation of the *Wu-men kan,* an important source book of Zen Buddhism.

# BIBLIOGRAPHY

SPIEGELBERG, FREDERIC. *The Religion of No-Religion* (Stanford, 1948). A profound and suggestive series of essays on the spiritual traditions of East and West, incorporating the author's *Alchemy as a Way of Salvation* (Stanford, 1945).

SUZUKI, DAISETZ T. (Trs.). *The Lankavatara Sutra* (London, 1932). One of the most important original sources of Mahayana Buddhism.

(Trs.). *Manual of Zen Buddhism* (Kyoto, 1935). An excellent anthology of source material for the study of Zen.

*Essays in Zen Buddhism.* 3 vols. (Luzac and Co., London, 1927, 1933 and 1934). This is by far the most important and extensive work on Zen in the English language.

*Introduction to Zen Buddhism* (London and New York, 1949). A readable and excellent summary.

*Studies in the Lankavatara Sutra* (G. Routledge and Sons, London, 1930).

*Zen and Japanese Culture* (New York, 1959). Contains some of his best and most profound work.

TAKAKUSU, JUNJIRO. *The Essentials of Buddhist Philosophy* (Honolulu, 1947). A most useful and often very profound compendium of Buddhist (esp. Mahayana) metaphysic. The author is unfortunately imperfectly versed in the Vedanta, and, in contrasting it with Buddhism, misrepresents it quite seriously. The ill-suited use of some of the terms of Western philosophy for Buddhist concepts may be overlooked, as his actual exposition of the latter is not affected thereby.

THIBAUT, G. (Trs.). *Vedanta Sutras.* 2 vols., with Shankara's Commentary, in the *Sacred Books of the East* (The Sacred Books of the East Series, London, 1890 and 1896).

WATTS, ALAN W. *The Spirit of Zen* (John Murray, London, 1948). A reprint of the 1936 edition. The sections on Mahayanist metaphysic and Zen meditation are to be taken with reservations.

*The Way of Zen* (New York, 1957).

*Beyond Theology* (New York, 1964).

*Behold the Spirit.* New Edition (New York, 1971).

WILHELM, RICHARD (Trs.). *The I Ching, or Book of Changes.* Third Edition (Princeton, N.J., 1967).

WILHELM, RICHARD and JUNG, C. G. *The Secret of the Golden*

*Flower* (Kegan Paul and Co., London and New York, 1931). Wilhelm's translation of the *T'ai I Chin Hua Tsung Chih,* a Taoist-Buddhist text on Chinese *yoga,* with a suggestive commentary by Jung.

WOODROFFE, JOHN. *Shakti and Shakta* (Luzac and Co., London and Madras, 1929). A very scarce but rather fine series of essays on Hindu *Tantra.* Particularly to be recommended for its discussion of the meaning of *maya.*

YAMPOLSKY, PHILIP (Trs.). *The Platform Sutra of the Sixth Patriarch* (New York, 1967).

ZIMMER, HEINRICH. *The King and the Corpse* (New York, 1948).

*Myths and Symbols in Indian Art and Civilization* (New York, 1946). Both the above contain some first-rate essays on the interpretation of Hindu mythology, with valuable notes by Coomaraswamy.

*Philosophies of India* (New York, 1951).

# INDEX

# INDEX

# INDEX

## VINTAGE WORKS OF SCIENCE AND PSYCHOLOGY

## VINTAGE FICTION, POETRY, AND PLAYS